Introduction

The Science Coordination Group was set up with the aim of producing specialised material for National Curriculum Science. This book provides concise coverage of the Programme of Study for the National Curriculum at Key Stage Two.

Our books exhibit several key features which set them apart from the rest.

1) Careful and relevant explanations

We work hard to give concise and carefully written details on each topic, supported by clear, informative and rather jolly diagrams.

2) Deliberate use of humour and relaxed language

We consider the humour to be an essential part of this Study Book. It's there to keep the reader interested and entertained, and we're sure that it greatly assists their learning. Our unique colourful style has proved extremely popular and successful in our KS3 and KS4 books, and we believe it gets the information across better than anything else.

3) Carefully Matched to the KS2 Programme of Study

This book provides a resource for teachers and pupils to use for teaching and learning Science at KS2, whether or not they are directly following the exemplar scheme of work recently set out by the Qualifications and Curriculum Authority (Autumn 1998)
This book will also be invaluable to teachers and pupils in Year 6 preparing for the dreaded SATs at age 11. Material is arranged so that pupils can revise topics across several units of work. Each page or double page spread has a 'Top Tips' box which gives pupils useful hints on learning the material and reminds them of the main points on the page. Summary questions are provided at the end of each section so that pupils can check their progress. The idea is to learn and enjoy...

Contents

Life Processes and Living Things

Materials and their Properties

Physical Processes

Experimental and Investigative Science

Published by Coordination Group Publications
Typesetting and layout by The Science Coordination Group
Illustrations by: Sandy Gardner, e-mail: zimkit@aol.com
                    and Coordination Group Publications

Contributors:
Paddy Gannon
Philip Goodyear
Tony Laukaitis
Lesley Lockhart

Also thanks to CorelDRAW for providing one or two jolly bits of clipart.

Printed by Hindson Print, Newcastle upon Tyne.

Looking at Life

What all Living Things Do

1) Although all *living things* look different from each other, they *all do the seven life processes.*
2) Animals and plants are called *living organisms.*
3) Something is only *alive* if it does all seven processes.

The Seven Life Processes — Remember "MRS NERG"

1) M - Move — even just a bit

Animals usually move their *whole bodies*, moving from one place to another.
Leaves turn *towards light*. Roots *grow down* into the soil.

2) R - Reproduce — living things have offspring

Animals have babies.
New *plants* grow from seeds

3) S - Sensitive — responding to changes

Living things *notice changes* in their surroundings and *react* to them.
Plants grow towards light. A dog smells its food and runs towards it.

4) N - Nutrition — taking in food

Food is used to provide energy.
Green plants make their own food using sunlight.
Animals eat plants or other animals.

5) E - Excrete — you have to get rid of waste

Waste substances must be *removed* from the body.
Both plants and animals need to get rid of *waste gas* and *water*.

6) R - Respire — living organisms are active

Plants and animals use the *oxygen* in the air to *turn food into energy* for muscles.

7) G - Grow — it's all geting bigger

Seedlings grow into bigger plants.
Babies grow into adults.

Are you alive — take a life test...

If it's alive it does all *seven* of those *life processes*, whether it's a plant, a person or even a penguin. So do you know what the seven are yet? If that was a "no" look back, and remember that the first letters of the words spell *"MRS NERG"* — let that help you for an easy life — and make sure you know what they *mean* too.

Dead or Alive

Living things are made From Cells

All *living organisms* are made up of really really tiny things called *cells*. Your body is made from millions of cells. Most cells are far too small to see with the naked eye, so a *microscope* lets you see cells.

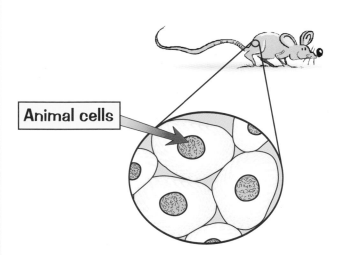

Animal cells

Plant cells

Dead things are still made From Cells

Things like *wood* or *leather* used to be part of a living thing, so they're still made of cells.

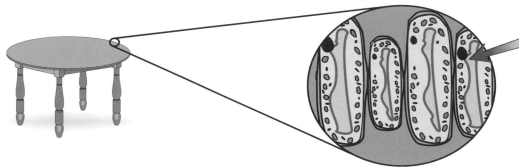

Dead plant cells

Things that Never Lived are NOT made From Cells

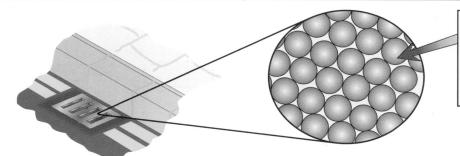

Not cells — these bits are smaller than cells and are called *particles*

Cells are Cool — well you're made of them..

Every living thing is made of *cells*, you and me included, so it's vital you know about them. Don't forget that not everything is made from cells, but only things that are *alive* or were *once alive*. You don't have to know a lot about cells, just that they're there.

Summary Questions For Section One

So we're the same as plants, worms and mice. As far as life processes go, yes! And how many life processes are there? *Seven* of course — think of *MRS NERG*, she'll help you remember them. You also have to know *how* they are carried out — *LEARNING* will help there. And don't forget *cells*, *plants* and the *human body* too. This might sound like a lot to learn, but practice these questions over and over until you can do them all and you'll be fine (so *NO* leaving out the *HARD ONES*). Okay then — there is no time like the present, so get started...

1) Name the seven life processes.
2) What must you remember to help learn the seven life processes?
3) How can you tell if something is *alive*?

4) Is the cartoon above true or false?
5) In what way are plants and animals *similar*?
6) Which life process brings *new life* to the world?
7) When you respire, what *gas* is used to turn *food* into *energy*?
8) Which life process means, "waste substances are *removed* from the body"?
9) All living things are *sensitive* and *grow*. What does this mean?
10) What tiny things are all *organisms* made up of?
11) What are *dead* things made up of?
12) True or false: *"things that never lived are made up of tiny particles but not cells"*.
13) In the list below say whether the thing is *living*, *dead*, or *never lived*.
   a) A dog running down the road?
   b) A wooden chair?
   c) An iron spade?
   d) A leather jacket?
   e) A cotton jumper?
   f) An apple on a tree?
   g) A rotting cabbage?
   h) A glass bottle?

Plants

Built to do the Seven Life Processes

There are *4 main parts to a plant*, all made to do those seven life processes (see P.1).

1) *Flowers*

— necessary for *REPRODUCTION*.

They have *colour* and *smell* to attract insects.
They make *pollen (male sex cells)* which join to the eggs *(female sex cells)*. Part of the flower dies and becomes the new fruit with *seeds*.

2) *Leaves*

— necessary for *NUTRITION (feeding)*.

The *green chlorophyll* in the leaves uses sunlight to change carbon dioxide gas and water into *food* — this is called *photosynthesis*.
Leaves are therefore important for *NUTRITION (feeding)* and *EXCRETION (getting rid of waste)*.

3) *Stem*

— necessary to *HOLD and MOVE* the plant up towards the light.

It carries *water* and *minerals* from the *roots* to the *rest of the plant*.

4) *Roots*

— these *ANCHOR THE PLANT* to the ground so it doesn't blow away.

They have *root hairs* to *soak* in the *water* and *minerals* from the soil.
The roots are therefore necessary for *NUTRITION (feeding)*.

Root hairs

Plants — there's more to them than pretty flowers...

The name of the game here is to *learn* everything on the page — there's no easy way to say it I'm afraid. Take *one* part of the plant at a time and see which of the life processes it's built to do. Then *cover up* the bit under the heading and see how much you can *remember*. Enjoy.

Nutrition

Animals have to *move* and *search* for their food, but green plants must stay in *one place* and make their *food*... which is really clever.

Green Plants make Food using Sunlight

This clever trick is called *Photosynthesis*. It might sound complicated, but it's just a long name.

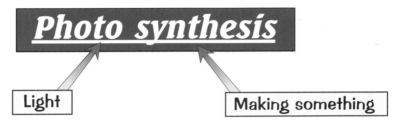

1) *PHOTOSYNTHESIS* means using *light* to make food.

2) Photosynthesis takes place in *green leaves*.

3) *Chlorophyll* in the green leaves uses *LIGHT* to change *CARBON DIOXIDE* gas and *WATER* into food and oxygen.

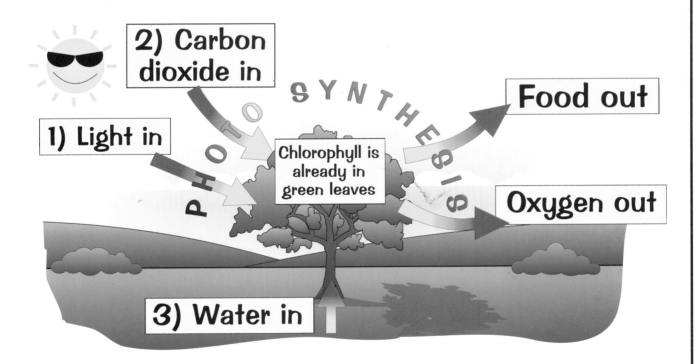

Making food without moving — that's just lazy...

Imagine it — all the food you could ever want, just by sitting there *sun bathing* and taking in *water* and *carbon dioxide*, which in this country are always available — well, the sun is sometimes. I reckon that has to be the easiest life ever. *Photosynthesis* and *chlorophyll* are pretty long words, but don't be afraid of them. Photosynthesis means using light to make something, and chlorophyll is the *green stuff* in the leaves that does it.

Growth

Growing Healthy Plants

1) Plants make their own *food (sugars)* using air *(carbon dioxide)* and water.

2) But to be fighting fit and healthy they need *other substances* as well.

3) Plants take in *minerals* which are in the *water* in the soil using their roots.

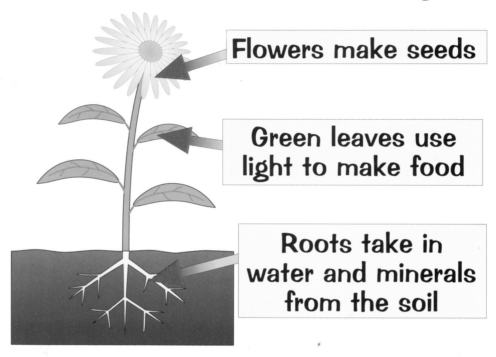

Flowers make seeds

Green leaves use light to make food

Roots take in water and minerals from the soil

Minerals are Very Important for the Plant

1) They need nutrients like minerals to keep the plant growing *strong* and *healthy*.

2) Plants grow using *minerals (goodies)* in the soil.

3) If plants don't get all the *minerals* they need they go yellow, pale, thin or spindly.

4) *Fertilisers* (plant food) are added to the soil to make sure the plant gets all the *nutrients* it needs.

Get back to your roots — take in all this...

Remember, the plant doesn't get food from the soil — it makes all the food it needs in the leaves. Don't forget, though, the plant needs *water*, or it'll wilt. As if that wasn't enough, plants need *minerals*, too. Remember what plants *look like* if they're growing in poor soil, and what we give them to make them *perk up* a bit.

Parts of a Flower

A plant won't live for ever, so it has to make *new plants*. This is called *reproduction*.

The Reproductive Organs are inside the Flower

1) The job of making new plants is done by the *flowers*.

2) The flowers contain the pollen and eggs which make seeds.

3) The *seeds* grow into new plants.

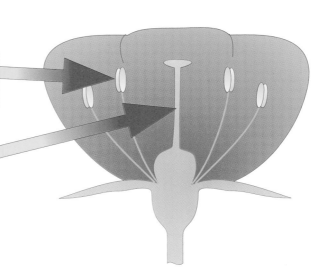

The stamens contain pollen grains

The carpel contains the eggs

The Flower contains the Male and Female Parts

Anther contains pollen

Filament holds the anther up

MALE: STAMEN

Stigma is sticky to catch pollen

Style holds the stigma up

Ovary contains eggs (also called ovules)

FEMALE: CARPEL

Not just smelling nice, you know...

Male and female parts in a *plant* sounds odd, but that's nature for you, always full of surprises. You need to know *which* are the *male* parts of a flower, which are the *female* parts and what they do. You've also got to *recognise* them on a diagram, so learn what they *look* like. Remember, it's all about making a *new plant*, and the plant needs to make a *seed* to do that.

SECTION TWO — PLANTS

Pollination and Fertilisation

Pollen Landing on the Sticky Stigma is called Pollination

Getting the pollen to the female is pretty straightforward.
There's two exciting ways it can happen. Read on...

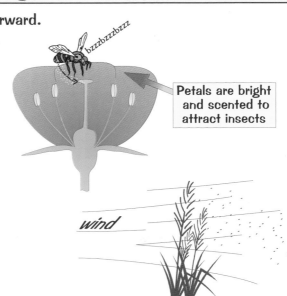

1) Some flowers are *pollinated by insects*. Insects are attracted to the flowers by their *scent* and *bright coloured* petals. They look for *nectar* and get covered in *pollen* and *carry it* to the female stigma.

Petals are bright and scented to attract insects

2) Some flowers are pollinated by the *wind*. The *long male stamens* are blown about and the pollen is carried to the *stigma*.

wind

Fertilisation takes place after Pollination

1) After pollination the *pollen* grain (*male sex cell*) and the *egg* (*female sex cell*) JOIN.
2) When the pollen and the egg join a seed is made — this is called FERTILISATION.

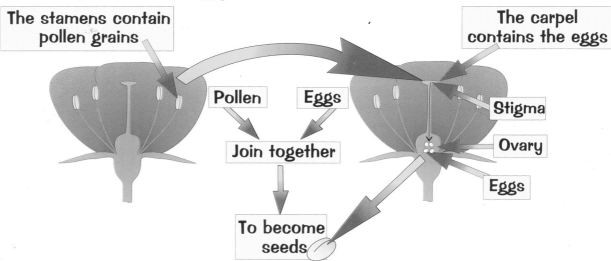

The stamens contain pollen grains

The carpel contains the eggs

Pollen | Eggs

Join together

Stigma

Ovary

Eggs

To become seeds

Pollination = Getting the Pollen to the Stigma

Fertilisation = Joining of the Pollen and the Egg

Pollination — gets right up my nose...a tissue

You need to know what has to happen for the plant to make a seed. Remember that the *pollen* has to get to the *female* part of the plant first, and then the *pollen* and the *egg* have to *join up*. Don't forget the *two* ways that the pollen makes its way to the stamen. Flowers using these two methods tend to look a bit different from each other — see if you can remember how...

How the Human Body Works

The Body does Four Basic Things

1) Your body takes in FOOD and OXYGEN gas from the air.

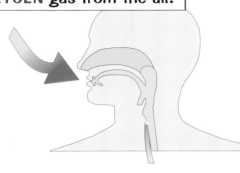

3) Body cells use the food we eat and the oxygen we breath in to get energy. Waste substances are given back to the blood.

2) Blood carries food and oxygen to the BODY CELLS.

4) Blood carries the waste to the lungs and kidneys to be removed

Organs are Special Parts which keep the Body Working

Getting stuff into the body

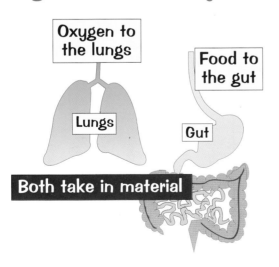

Oxygen to the lungs

Food to the gut

Lungs

Gut

Both take in material

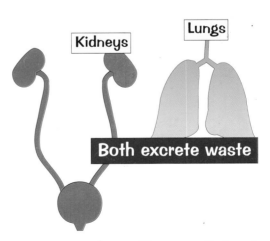

Kidneys

Lungs

Both excrete waste

Getting stuff out of the body

Stuff goes in, and stuff comes out...

Everything that the body does comes down to this: stuff goes in and stuff comes out. *Four* labelled points to learn and a nice diagram to show you how it all works. One last thing, remember what sort of *waste* the body makes and *how* it gets rid of it. Learn and enjoy. ☺

Skeleton

You have a Skeleton on the inside of your Body

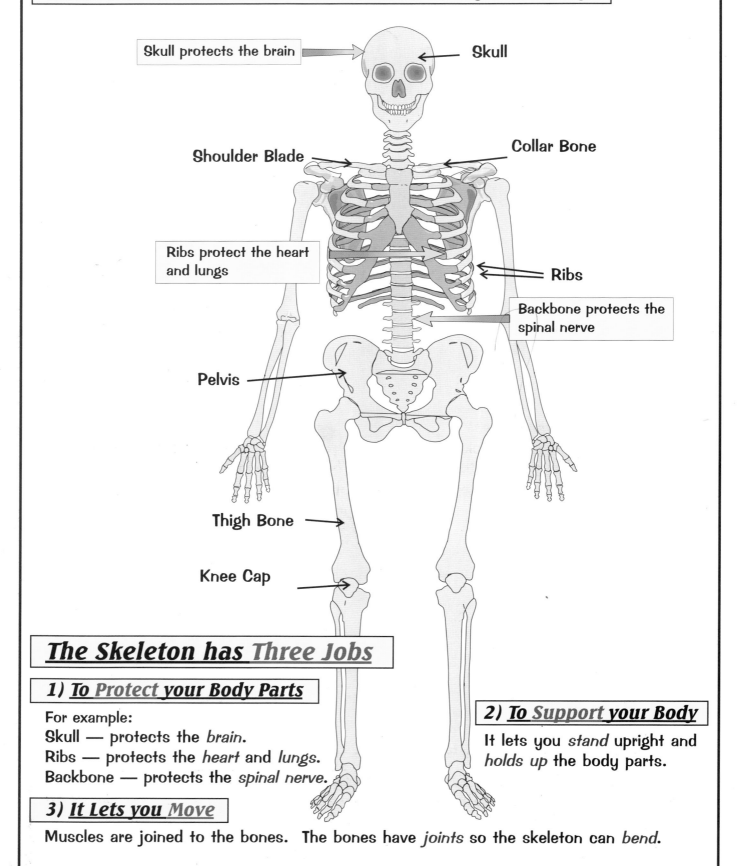

Skull protects the brain

Skull

Shoulder Blade

Collar Bone

Ribs protect the heart and lungs

Ribs

Backbone protects the spinal nerve

Pelvis

Thigh Bone

Knee Cap

The Skeleton has Three Jobs

1) To Protect your Body Parts

For example:
Skull — protects the *brain*.
Ribs — protects the *heart* and *lungs*.
Backbone — protects the *spinal nerve*.

2) To Support your Body

It lets you *stand* upright and *holds up* the body parts.

3) It Lets you Move

Muscles are joined to the bones. The bones have *joints* so the skeleton can *bend*.

Movement

Muscles and Joints allow Movement

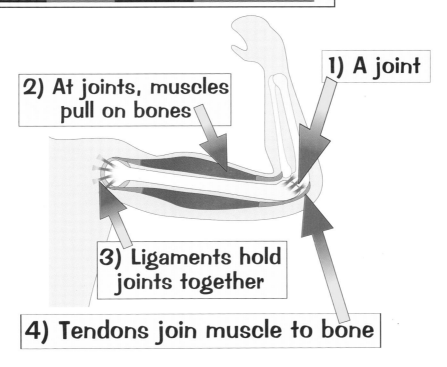

2) At joints, muscles pull on bones

1) A joint

3) Ligaments hold joints together

4) Tendons join muscle to bone

Joints and Muscles

1) Muscles always work in *pairs*.
2) To move a joint, one muscle gets *SHORTER (contracts)* and *pulls* the bone while the other muscle gets *LONGER* and *relaxes (but is stretched)*.
3) To move the joint back to where it started, the relaxed muscle then contracts.

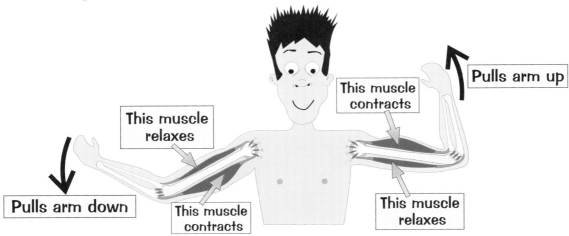

This muscle relaxes

This muscle contracts

Pulls arm up

Pulls arm down

This muscle contracts

This muscle relaxes

This is alright — only got to learn the bare bones...

There's three fantastic reasons why you've got a skeleton — and you need to know 'em. Make sure you learn how we move our body. Remember that muscles work in *pairs* and one *relaxes* while the other *contracts*. It might seem a bit tricky, but think about it, and you should see how it works. Try watching the muscles in your arm as you move it up and down.

SECTION THREE — THE HUMAN BODY

Circulation

Blood and the Heart make up the Circulatory System

Circulatory system sounds like city traffic, but it's your *blood*, your *blood vessels* and your *heart* — and it's really important. Learn these three facts:

1) Blood moves *food* and *oxygen* around the body.
2) It *circulates* around the body through three kinds of blood vessel: *arteries*, *veins* and *capillaries*.
3) The heart pumps the blood through the blood vessels so food and oxygen can get to all the *cells* of the body.

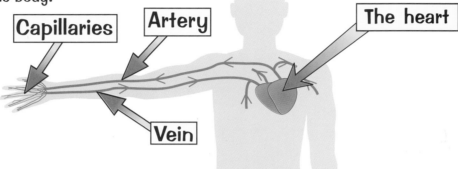

Capillaries Artery The heart

Vein

Arteries — carry blood away from the heart to the body cells.

Veins — carry blood away from the cells back to the heart.

Capillaries — allow food and gases to move in and out of the blood.

The Heart Pumps the Blood Around the Body

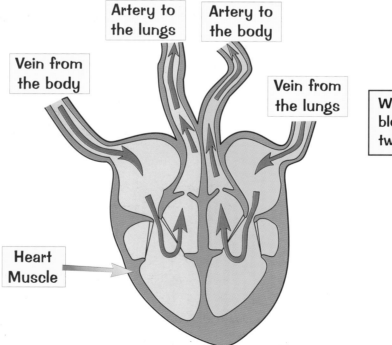

Artery to the lungs Artery to the body

Vein from the body

Vein from the lungs

When the heart beats, blood is pumped out of two arteries.

Heart Muscle

1) One *artery* takes the blood to the lungs where it picks up *oxygen* gas and goes back to the heart.
2) When it does this, it lets out *carbon dioxide* gas into the lungs, which is *breathed out*.
3) The other artery then takes the blood with *oxygen* and *food* to all the body cells.
4) Veins *return* the blood to the *heart*.
5) The heart is inside the *rib cage*, which protects it.

The Lungs and Breathing

The Lungs are big Air Sacs

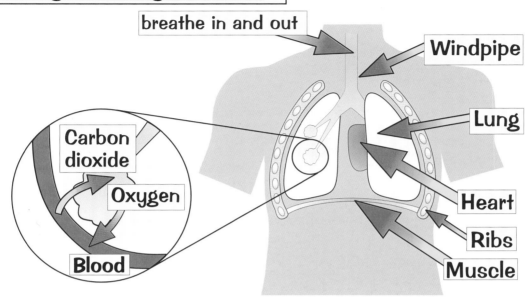

breathe in and out

Windpipe

Lung

Carbon dioxide

Oxygen

Blood

Heart

Ribs

Muscle

1) The lungs are like two *spongy bags* filled with millions of tiny air sacs.
2) Each lung has a good *blood supply*.
3) It's the job of the lungs to give *oxygen* to the blood and remove *carbon dioxide*.
4) This happens every time you breathe *in* and *out*.

When you Exercise, your Muscles need more Oxygen and Food

Heart beats can be felt as a pulse around the body — e.g. the wrist and the neck.

1) The harder you work, the more *energy* your muscles need.

2) The heart *beats* faster and you *breathe* faster, to get food and oxygen to the muscles.

3) It beats at about 70 beats per minute in adults, but faster in children.

4) The *fitter* you are the *slower* your heart has to pump and the quicker your heart returns to normal, after exercise.

Heart beat — it's the rhythm of life....

The heart is a big *pump* that moves our *blood* around our body. You need to know why we need the blood to be pumped round our *whole* body all the time. There's a few new words here that you'll need to learn. Your heart beats faster after you've been exercising because it's had to work harder to pump more blood round. Try measuring your pulse when you're sat down, then measuring it again after exercise in your PE lessons.

SECTION THREE — THE HUMAN BODY

18

Teeth

Teeth help you to *cut*, *tear* and *crush* your food before you swallow it. Humans are *omnivores* (they eat plants and animals) and their teeth are designed to eat most types of food.

Humans have Three Types of Teeth

MOLARS: Back teeth for *crushing* and *grinding* food.

CANINES *(Fangs):*
In meat-eating animals like cats and dogs they are long and sharp and are used for *stabbing* and *gripping* food.

INCISORS:
Front teeth are for *snipping* and *cutting* food.

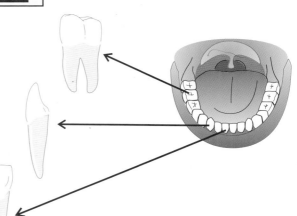

Humans have Two Sets of Teeth during their Lives

1) MILK teeth (about 20 teeth)
Used from six months old to about 5 years old.

2) PERMANENT teeth (about 32 teeth)
Used from five years old to...
...depends how you look after them.

Teeth are different in other Animals

CARNIVORES (meat eaters) have teeth suited to killing other animals and tearing flesh. Canines are long and pointed for holding and gripping flesh. Molars can crack and crush bones.

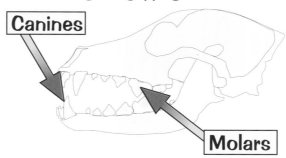

Canines

Molars

HERBIVORES (plant eaters) have teeth suited to eat plants. Incisors cut grass off. Molars grind the grass as the jaws move side to side.

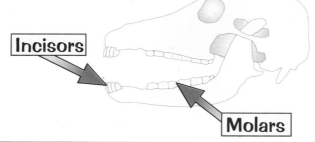

Incisors

Molars

Teeth

Bacteria cause Tooth Decay

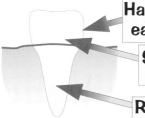

Hard enamel outside is eaten away by plaque

Soft dentine inside

Root in gum

1) Sugar left in the mouth after eating food is eaten by *bacteria*.

2) The bacteria form a white sticky slime covering the teeth called *PLAQUE*.

3) The plaque contains *acid* which rots away the tooth enamel and weakens teeth.

Four ways to Look after your Teeth

1) *Brushing* teeth at least twice a day helps remove plaque.

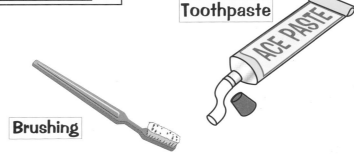

Toothpaste

Brushing

2) *Flossing* the teeth also helps remove plaque and bits of food which bacteria feed on.

3) Drink *water* which contains *fluoride* — some scientists think this helps to keep teeth strong.

Water

4) Tooth decay is also prevented by visiting the *dentist*.

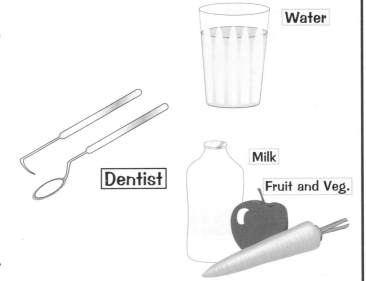

Dentist

Milk

Fruit and Veg.

5) Eating the *correct foods* (not so many sweeties, plenty of carrots, drink milk).

Get your teeth into this lot.....

What a fantastic double page on choppers — lots of jolly pictures to make learning about teeth *dead easy*. But you really should know all about this already. Anyone with any sense knows how to look after their teeth, you'd miss them if they weren't there. Now smile....

Life Cycle of a Human

Reproduction produces Babies

1) Animals do not live for ever. More must be made to take the place of those that die.

2) More animals are produced by *reproduction*.

3) A baby grows from a *tiny cell* in its mother.

4) The tiny cell is made when an *egg* inside its mother is fertilised by a *sperm* from the father.

Egg   Sperm

5) When the egg is *fertilised* an *embryo* starts to develop.

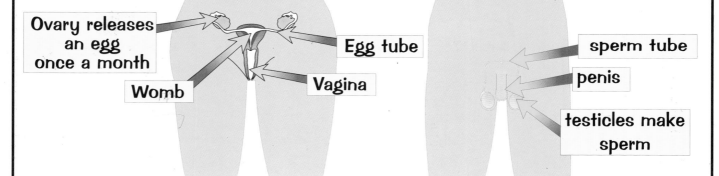

Ovary releases an egg once a month

Egg tube

Womb

Vagina

sperm tube

penis

testicles make sperm

Growing from Egg to Birth

1) When an egg is fertilised, it grows into a tiny *ball of cells* called an *embryo*.

2) It grows inside the *womb* of the mother and becomes a *baby*.

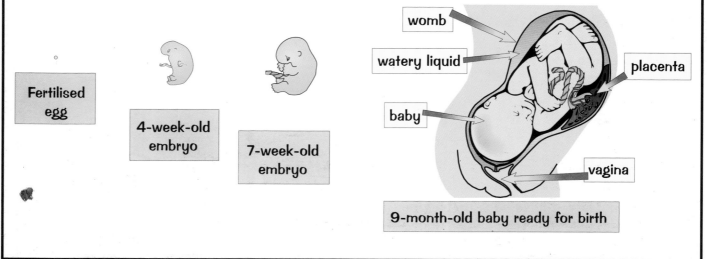

Fertilised egg

4-week-old embryo

7-week-old embryo

womb

watery liquid

placenta

baby

vagina

9-month-old baby ready for birth

Life Cycle of a Human

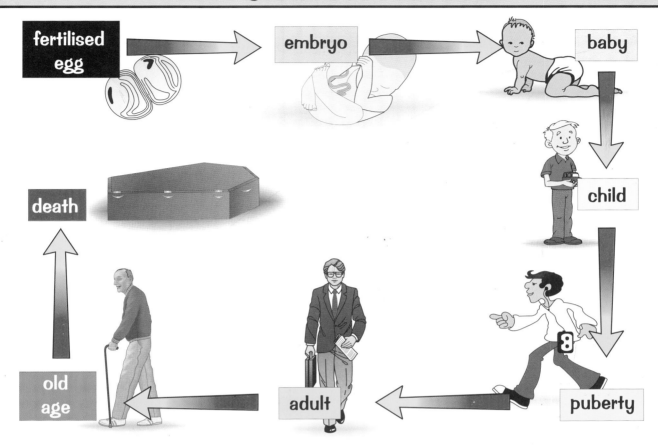

Puberty *is when the Body* Develops

1) Puberty happens between 10 and 18 years old.
2) In puberty the bodies of boys and girls begin to change.

Girls:

1) *Hair* starts to grow on their bodies.
2) *Breasts* develop and *hips* widen.
3) *Ovaries* start to release *egg cell.*
4) A monthly loss of blood happens. This comes from the lining of the womb which breaks down if an egg is not fertilised. This is called *menstruation* and is often known as a *period.*

Boys:

1) *Hair* starts to grow on their bodies.
2) *Hair* also starts to grow on their *faces.*
3) *Testicles* start producing *sperm.*

Life cycles — from cradle to grave, by bike.

The thing to remember here is that *new* animals have to be born, or there won't be any left when the old ones die. Remember, animals *change* as they grow. Tiny babies are totally dependent on their parents for everything, but you can do quite a bit for yourself, I should hope. You need to know about the changes that happen to both boys and girls when you go through puberty.

Healthy Living

To stay fit and keep that natural glow of health you need to:

1) *Eat* sensibly;   2) Take *exercise* regularly;   3) Avoid unnecessary *health risks*.

The Right Food is important for a Healthy Body

1) You need to eat a *balanced diet*.
2) A balanced diet is a *mixture* of these *seven* food types:

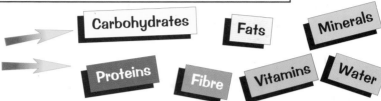

Food group	Why you need them	Which Foods have them
Carbohydrates 1) Starches	For energy	Bread Pasta Cereals Rice
Carbohydrates 2) Sugars		Biscuits Cakes Sweets
Proteins	For cell growth and repair	Fish Meat Milk Eggs
Fats	For energy	Milk, Cheese Butter Cooking oil Meat
Vitamins and minerals	For healthy cells	Fruit Vegetables Dairy products
Fibre	Helps food move through the gut	Whole grain bread Cereals Fruit Vegetables
Water	70% of the body is water	Drinks (Some foods)

Exercise is important for a Healthy Body

Because:

1) it strengthens the *muscles*.

2) it develops the *lungs*.

3) it helps body *co-ordination* develop (*so you can catch and throw*).

4) it uses up *food* for energy and may prevent the body getting fat.

5) it can help you *sleep* at night time.

Healthy Living

Taking Health Risks can Damage the Body

Smoking

This causes heart attacks, blocked arteries, lung cancer and breathing problems. Tobacco contains nicotine which cause addiction.

Solvents

Sniffing glue and paint is extremely dangerous. It damages the brain and is addictive.

ESASTICK

GLUE

Alcohol

In small amounts it is not as harmful as smoking, but it slows down your reactions. Heavy drinking damages the liver, heart and stomach. It causes your blood pressure to rise.

Drugs

These can be dangerous if misused. Many are addictive They can cause damage to the brain (or worse).

Live long — and prosper....

You need to know about staying *healthy*: eat the right food stuffs, keep well clear of dangerous drugs and solvents, realize that smoking and drinking damage the body, do enough exercise. Don't forget *why* all these things are good or bad for you.

Microbes and Disease

Microbes are Tiny Living Things

1) Microbes or *micro-organisms* can only be seen through a *microscope*.
2) There are millions of microbes in the *soil*, *air*, *water* and even the *human body*.
3) Some microbes are *USEFUL* and some are *DANGEROUS*.
4) Bacteria and viruses are *microbes*.

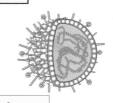

virus

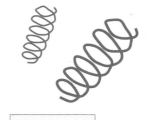

bacteria

The non-scientific word for these is *"germ"*

Helpful Microbes do Important Jobs

2) Bacteria rot down dead organisms and put nutrients in the soil for plants to help them grow.

1) Bacteria which help make vinegar, cheese and yoghurt.

3) Yeast is a microbe: it's used to make bread and beer.

(Gee — I'm glad the world's not cluttered with dead bodies!)

Harmful Microbes can cause Disease

1) They cause *disease* and *illness*: flu, colds, measles, chicken pox, Aids, tetanus, etc.
2) Microbes cause *tooth decay*.

Four Ways of Spreading Disease

1) From coughs and sneezes

2) From touching infected people or objects

3) From insect bites

4) From infected food

SECTION THREE — THE HUMAN BODY

Fighting Disease

In the Kitchen — Be sensible with Food

1) Keep food covered.

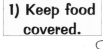

2) Store food in a fridge.

3) Heat food properly when cooking.

4) Store raw meat away from cooked meat.

5) Preserve foods properly — take away water and air.

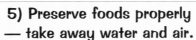

Dried Foods   Tinned Foods   Pickled Foods   Salted foods

At home — Be Sensible with Personal Hygiene

1) Wash your hands after going to the toilet.

2) Don't sneeze or cough over people.

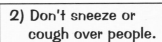

At the Doctors — Medicines are used to Fight Microbes

Medicines called vaccinations and antibiotics are taken as pills or injected to fight microbes that cause illness.

Microbes and disease — my favourite topic....

It's important that you know how diseases are caused, it'll help stop you from getting ill for one thing. Like it says, fighting disease in the home is all about being *sensible*. Remember that microbes breed very fast in things that are *warm* and open to the *air*. Don't forget, not all microbes are *harmful* — some are actually very *useful* to us.

Summary Questions For Section Three

This is one mighty section — *all* you ever wanted to know about yourself and more. Now all you need to do is *learn it*! Once more no expense has been spared in preparing some brilliant questions. Keep going over them *again* and *again*. They test your knowledge on the basic facts. Now then let's get on with it, shall we?

1) *Draw* the body outline shown opposite :
  Draw in the following *organs:* — brain, lungs, heart, liver, stomach, intestines, kidneys, bladder.

2) What two important things do humans need to take in to stay alive?
3) Name two organs which remove waste material.
4) Where is the skeleton on a human being?
5) Give *three reasons* why you have a skeleton.
6) What *joins* the muscles to bones?
7) What *holds* the bones together at the *joints*?
8) Muscles always work in pairs. When one muscle contracts, what does the *other muscle* do?
9) Name the *three types* of blood vessel in the body.
10) Which type of *blood vessel* lets gases and food move in and out of it?
11) What organ pumps blood around the body?
12) Which *gas* does blood *take* from the lungs and which gas does it *give* to the lungs?
13) Which type of blood vessel carries blood *away* from the *heart*?
14) What is the *name* of the tube that carries *gases* in and out of the lungs?
15) What is a *pulse*: is it A) a vegetable B) a heart beat or C) a blood vessel?
16) *How many* beats does an adult's heart make in *one minute* (when resting)?
17) What are the *three* main types of *teeth*?
18) Say *which type* of teeth does the job:
  a) snipping/cutting b) crushing/grinding c) tearing/gripping.
19) What is the *difference* in the diet of these animal groups:
  a)omnivore b) carnivore c) herbivore?
20) What is the *first set* of teeth in humans called?
21) What is *plaque* and what *causes* it?
22) What is the *outside* of a tooth called: enamel or dentine?
23) Give *four ways* of preventing tooth decay.
24) Name the main *stages* of the life cycle of a human being.
25) What happens to a boy's and a girl's body during *puberty*?
26) What is *menstruation*?
27) Name the *seven* food groups.
28) Which *two* food groups provide energy?
29) Give *three reasons* why exercise is important.
30) Smoking and alcohol are health risks. Which causes *lung cancer*, which damages the *liver*?
31) What is the *non-scientific* name often given to microbes?
32) Name *two groups* of microbes.
33) Give *three advantages* of microbes.
34) Name *three diseases* caused by microbes.
35) Give three *safety tips* for handling food in the kitchen.
36) Give two safety tips for *personal hygiene*, to prevent microbes spreading from person to person.
37) Name two groups of *medicines* used by doctors to fight microbes.

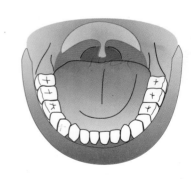

Sorting Living Things Out

Because there are so many varied *(different)* plants and animals, scientists keep dividing them into smaller groups. They look for *differences* and *similarities* to put the plants and animals into *groups*.

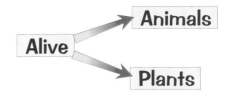

Alive → Animals
Alive → Plants

Animal Groups

All the animals in the world can be put into one of two groups 1) Vertebrates or 2) Invertebrates.

VERTEBRATES are animals with a backbone

Fish
breathe with gills
lay eggs in water
have fins and scales
body temp. changes
e.g. trout, shark, salmon

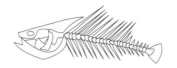

Amphibians
born with gills that turn into lungs
lay eggs in water
damp skin
body temp. changes
e.g. frog, toad, newt

Reptiles
lungs
lay eggs on land
dry scaly skin
body temp. changes
e.g. alligator, snake, crocodile, tortoise

Birds
lungs
lay eggs with hard shells
feathers
steady body temp.
e.g. penguin, ostrich, falcon

Mammals
lungs
babies born live
body hair or fur
steady body temp.
feed babies milk
e.g. dog, whale, lion, seal, bat

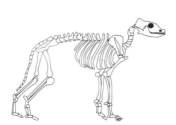

Vertebrates — spine chilling stuff...

There's quite a lot of information here. Look at *one* group at a time and learn the things that the animals in that group have got. The pictures will help it make sense. See how you can *divide* the animals up by asking *questions* like "does it lay eggs?". That's good practice for later.

Invertebrates

INVERTEBRATES are animals with no backbone

worm

centipede

butterfly

tarantula

wasp

crab

Invertebrates are also divided into groups. Each group shares similar characteristics.
Here are three groups:

1) Insects

For example: butterflies, beetles, flies, ants

Three body parts

Six legs

2) Arachnids

For example: spiders, scorpions

Two body parts

Eight legs

3) Molluscs

For example: snails, slugs, octopus

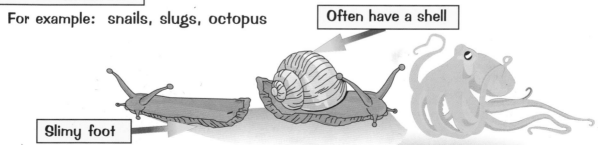

Often have a shell

Slimy foot

Learn about invertebrates — come out of your shell...

You can see that there's a lot of very different animals in the *invertebrate* group. Ones with hard shells, soft slimy ones, ones without legs — lovely. The thing to remember is that the *similar* ones are put into a group *together*. All the animals *without a backbone* then go into the big group called *invertebrates*.

SECTION FOUR — VARIATION AND CLASSIFICATION

Plant Groups

Plant Groups

All the plants in the world can be put into one of two groups: *flowering plants (with flowers)* and *non-flowering plants (without flowers).*

Flowering Plants

Grasses

Cereals

Deciduous Trees

(these lose their leaves, e.g: Oak, Birch, Chestnut)

Garden shrubs

Non-Flowering Plants

Algae

(slime in a pond and seaweed are both algae)

Fungi

(Mushrooms, toadstools and mould)

Coniferous Trees

(they are ever green, keep their leaves and have cones, e.g. Pine.)

Ferns

(they make spores instead of seeds)

Fungi or a fun girl — you still gotta learn all this...

You can divide *all* the plants in the world into *two groups* by asking the question "does the plant have flowers?". The flowering plants can look very different to each other — grass, daisies, oak trees and wheat all have flowers, which you might not expect. There's even more variation between the non flowering plants. Don't forget, non flowering plants *don't* make seeds.

SECTION FOUR — VARIATION AND CLASSIFICATION

Using Keys

Keys Unlock Information

Scientists use keys to *identify* unknown plants or animals, (and also to get in and out of their houses...) A key is a series of *questions*, each with *two* possible answers. The answers lead you to the next question or will identify the unknown creature. It's all very clever, as you'll find out when you give it a try...

Three Top Tips for Using Keys

1) Take *one* creature at a time.

2) Start at (1) and go through the questions for *that creature only*.

3) *Follow* the *answers*. They lead you to the next question or will identify the creature.

Have a go at using this key. Identify which group each of these animals is in.

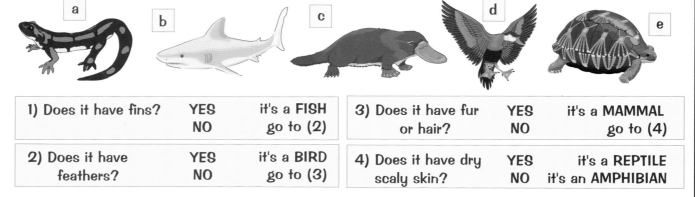

| 1) Does it have fins? | YES | it's a FISH |
| | NO | go to (2) |

| 3) Does it have fur or hair? | YES | it's a MAMMAL |
| | NO | go to (4) |

| 2) Does it have feathers? | YES | it's a BIRD |
| | NO | go to (3) |

| 4) Does it have dry scaly skin? | YES | it's a REPTILE |
| | NO | it's an AMPHIBIAN |

Answers: a = amphibian, b = fish, c = mammal, d = bird, e = reptile

Branched Keys

The key can be shown as a branched pattern. Same thing: just follow the line. Try this one.

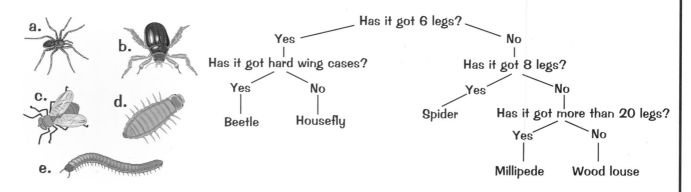

Answers: a = spider, b = beetle, c = housefly, d = wood louse, e = millipede.

Use keys — and unlock the answers...

You probably won't be expected to draw a key but you need to be able to *follow* one through and *identify* some unknown creatures. It's pretty *easy* really — just remember the *tips* above. Do remember to go through the key *step by step*, and *don't* just look at the pictures and *guess*.

SECTION FOUR — VARIATION AND CLASSIFICATION

Revision Summary For Section Four

Quite a slim section this one but don't be fooled. You'll need to know those nasty words and what they mean. For example: *vertebrates* and *invertebrates*. Remember that variation means "differences". Classification is all about grouping creatures that are similar in some way. You'll also need to know how to use a key. Okay, so you can let yourself into the house — but can you use a key to identify unknown creatures? Try out this one. Identify my unknown aliens! Good luck.

1) Use the *key* to find out the names of each alien creature.

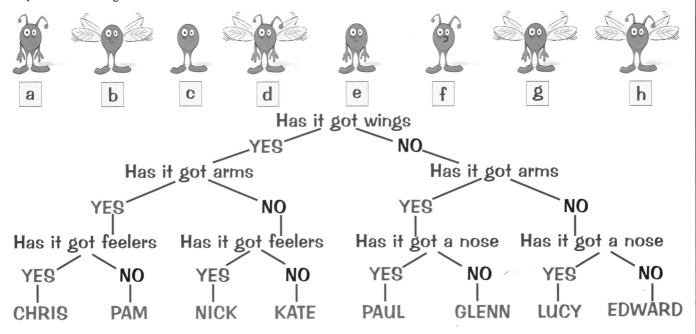

Has it got wings
YES / NO

Has it got arms (YES branch)
YES / NO

Has it got arms (NO branch)
YES / NO

Has it got feelers — YES: CHRIS, NO: PAM
Has it got feelers — YES: NICK, NO: KATE
Has it got a nose — YES: PAUL, NO: GLENN
Has it got a nose — YES: LUCY, NO: EDWARD

Answers: a = Glenn, b = Kate, c = Edward, d = Chris, e = Paul, f = Lucy, g = Pam, h = Nick

2) All living things can be placed into one of *two* groups. What are the two groups?
3) All animals can be placed into one of *two* groups. What are the two groups?
4) What does *vertebrate* mean?
5) Name the *five* vertebrate groups.
6) Name *three* invertebrate groups.
7) Say which of the five vertebrate groups each of these things goes with:
   (a) breathes with *gills* (b) has *feathers* (c) *dry scaly* skin (d) has *hair*
   (e) lays *eggs* in *water* but uses *lungs* to breathe when it's an *adult*.
8) Which two vertebrate groups have a *steady* body temperature?
9) Which three vertebrates groups have body temperatures the same as their *surroundings*?
10) Which vertebrate group has babies born *live* and feeds its babies with *milk*?
11) Which invertebrate group has 6 legs?
12) Give *two* differences between a spider and an ant.
13) All *plants* can be placed into one of *two* groups. What are the two groups?
14) Ferns are non-flowering plants that do not make seeds. *What* do they make?
15) What is the name of the trees that *do not* lose their leaves in winter?
16) Coniferous trees do not have flowers. *Where* are their seeds made?
17) What happens to the leaves of deciduous trees?
18) Name *two* deciduous trees.

Places to Live

Humans can live all over the world. We can do this because we are able to wear clothes and build houses suited for very different conditions — like Africa or the Arctic. Most plants and animals can only live in certain *environments* or surroundings — they can't change their clothes.

Where a Plant or Animal Lives is called its Habitat

The *habitat (where they live)* provides the plant or animal with *food* and *shelter*. The habitat also lets living things produce offspring *(make babies)* in a safe environment. E.g. Hedge, field or tree.

OTHER EXAMPLES:

The Frog in a Pond Habitat:

Lots of lovely *slugs* to eat.
Water for frog spawn.
Damp air so frog doesn't dry out.

A Bird in a Wood Habitat:

Plenty of materials to build a *nest*.
Feathers *camouflaged*.
Lots of juicy *worms* in the undergrowth.

Animals and Plants are Adapted to their Habitat

To help them to *survive* in their habitat, living things have developed *special features* to suit the place they live. These help them to survive in their habitat. Examples of adaptation:

The Otter

1) *Eyes* and *nostrils* can close under water.
2) *Feet* are webbed to help it move in water.
3) *Long whiskers* feel vibration in water help it find food.

The Squirrel

1) *Long claws* for gripping help it to climb.
2) *Strong teeth* for opening nuts.
3) *Bushy tail* for balance.

The Cactus

1) *Long roots* find water.
2) *Fleshy stems* store water.
3) *Thin needle leaves* don't lose water.

Food Chains

Animals which Eat Other Animals are Called Predators

The animals that the *predators* kill and eat are called their *prey*.

Predator

Prey

Examples of predators and prey:

Predators	Prey
Hawk	Thrush, Blue tit, Rabbit
Seal	Crab, Octopus, Penguin
Cod	Herring, Mackerel, Haddock

If One Part of the food chain changes — IT ALL CHANGES

Change one part of the food chain and the rest of the chain will be altered. In 1953, large numbers of rabbits were destroyed by a disease introduced into the environment by man.

Soon the countryside began to change. More plant life survived (fewer rabbits eating the plants) so more deer survived because there was more vegetation to eat. However, the number of foxes and hawks dropped because there were fewer rabbits to eat. Smaller animals such as mice and voles decreased in number because predators ate them instead of rabbits.

Who's eating who?...

Food chains are all about what eats what. Thinking of *plants* as *producers* and *animals* as *consumers* seems a bit odd to begin with, but if you remember that plants are the *only* ones who *produce* their *own food*, you'll get it sorted no trouble at all. Don't forget that *all* the animals are consumers, even the ones that get eaten, because they *don't* produce their own food. Remember that the arrow in a food chain doesn't mean *"eats"* — it means *"is food for"*. It's useful to imagine what would *happen* if you *changed* part of the food chain.

Food Chains

Obviously, in nature, you get different plants and different animals sharing the same habitat. Many animals eat more than one type of food. This is great for survival as an animal can eat different foods and not depend on just one thing. It also means it'll get a balanced diet. This all means that living things are usually part of several different food chains.

Food chains that are linked together make up what's called a *FOOD WEB*.

The Same Animal or Plant can be in lots of Food Chains

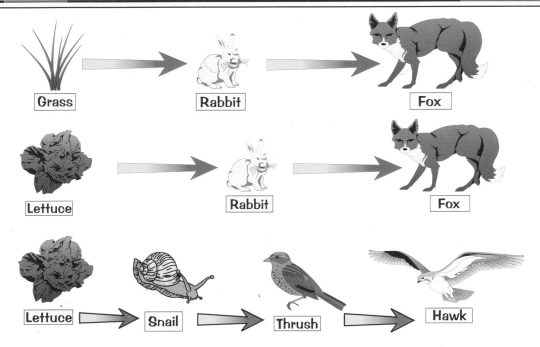

These can link up to make a *FOOD WEB*:

A Food Web

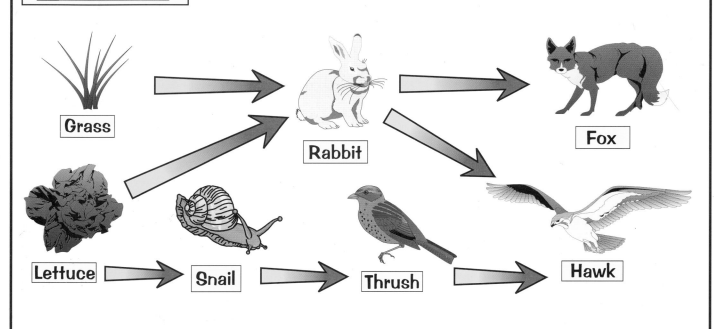

Food Webs

A Food Web Gives More Information about What Eats What

The food web below shows how different food chains might be linked together within a seashore habitat.

If the sea became polluted and the *shellfish* died off — this would alter the numbers of the other living things:

What happens when you change things

Look at the seashore food web. If there are fewer shellfish, then:

1) There will be more *seaweed*...   ....*because there's fewer shell fish to eat it.*
2) There will be fewer *starfish*...   ....*because there's less food for the starfish.*
3) There will be fewer *crabs*...   ....*because there's less food (shellfish) for the crabs and now they're being eaten more by the seagulls as there's fewer starfish.*

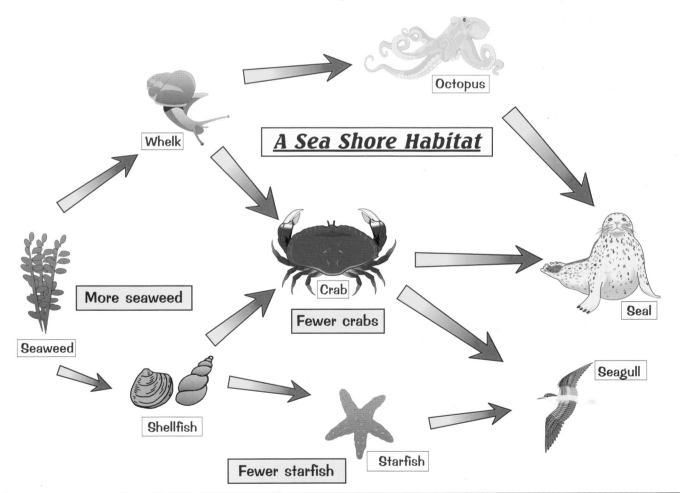

A Sea Shore Habitat

Octopus

Whelk

More seaweed

Seaweed

Crab

Fewer crabs

Seal

Shellfish

Seagull

Fewer starfish

Starfish

What a tangled web we weave...

Food webs really aren't a lot more complicated than food chains. They show a bit more of what's going on in real life, because *most* animals eat *more* than *one* kind of food. Working out what happens as you change things in a food web is rather tricky, though, but if you look at *each animal* and work out *what* it has to eat, you'll get there. You'll only really get asked about a simple *food chain* with three or four things in it.

Summary Questions for Section Five

This section is all about animals and plants *living together* in their *environment*. Many animals and plants have to *share* the *same habitat*. They all need to find food, shelter and somewhere to produce their offspring, and to do this without ending up as something else's lunch. To help living things survive in a competitive environment, they're all *very different*. They all have *special features* that let them live in different places and different ways. Work your way through the questions and look back at the section if you get stuck. *Good luck.*

1) What is the *name* of the *place* where a plant or an animal lives?
2) What does the habitat *provide* for an animal or plant?
3) Give two special features that an *otter* has so that it survives very well *in water*?
4) A squirrel has a *bushy tail*. How does this help it survive?
5) How is a cactus plant *adapted* to living in its *desert habitat*?
6) Give *one* adaptation that a seal has so it can live in *cold sea areas*.
7) Give *one* adaptation that a desert rat has so it can survive in a *desert habitat*.
8) Give three adaptations a *fish* has so it can survive in its water habitat.
9) Give three adaptations a *frog* has so it can survive in its water and land habitat.
10) Give three adaptations a *worm* has so it can survive in its soil habitat.
11) Give three adaptations a *woodlouse* has so it can survive under stones and bark.
12) Look at the *food chain* below then answer questions a) to i).

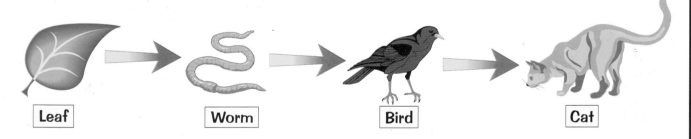

| Leaf | Worm | Bird | Cat |

a) Name the *producer*.
b) *How many* consumers are there?
c) Name a *consumer*.
d) Name the *prey* of the *cat*.
e) Name the *prey* of the *blackbird*.

f) What is the predator of the *worm*?
g) What is the predator of the *blackbird*?
h) Which animal has no predators?
i) Write down the name of a consumer that *eats another* consumer.

13) What does an arrow mean when used in a *food chain*?
14) Animals that are *eaten by* other animals are called what?
    (The answer is not, "unlucky")
15) Animals that *eat other* animals are called what?
16) What diagram is formed by *linking* different food chains together?

Fancy Words you need to Know

You probably don't believe this, but you really do need to know these — you need to test yourself by covering up the black bits and scribbling down what the coloured bit means, until you've got it right.

Artery   blood vessel carrying food and oxygen to the body cells.

Adapted   suited to the environment where the organism lives.

Balanced diet   a diet that gives the body the right amount of all the nutrients it needs.

Canines   pointed teeth that tear food.

Carbohydrate   food that gives the body energy — there are two types, starches and sugars.

Carpel   the female part of a flower.

Carnivore   animal that only eats other animals.

Cell   tiny parts that make up all living things.

Chlorophyll   the green stuff in plants that does photosynthesis and makes food.

Classification   grouping similar organisms together.

Consumer   something that consumes food and doesn't produce it, i.e. an animal.

Contract/Contraction   when a muscle gets shorter.

Dispersal/disperse   spreading seeds far away from the parent plant.

Excretion   getting rid of waste from the body.

Fertilisation/fertilise   when sperm joins with egg or pollen grain joins with ovule.

Food chain   shows what is food for what.

Food web   a lot of food chains linked up.

Germ   a non scientific word for microbe.

Germination/germinate   when a seed starts to grow.

Habitat   where an organism lives.

Heart beat   the heart pumps blood out.

Herbivore   an animal that only eats plants.

Incisors   teeth that cut food.

Key   a set of questions that help you identify an unknown animal.

Life cycle   the stages an organism goes through right from fertilisation to death.

Microbe/micro-organism   a very tiny living thing.

Minerals   needed by plants to help them grow.

Molars   teeth that grind food.

Muscles   pull on bones and make you move.

Nutrients   chemicals that organisms need to grow.

Nutrition   getting food in order to grow.

Organ   part of the body that has a special job.

Organism   a living thing, animal or plant.

Ovary   where eggs are made.

Photosynthesis   making food from carbon dioxide and water — needs chlorophyll and sunlight.

Plant food   minerals we give to a plant to help it to grow better — the plant makes its own food.

Pollen   the male part that goes to make a new seed.

Pollination/pollinate   getting pollen to the stigma.

Predator   an animal that eats other animals.

Prey   an animal killed and eaten by a predator.

Producer   an organism that makes its own food, i.e a plant.

Protein   food that builds muscle.

Puberty   when the body changes and develops between 10 and 18 years old.

Pulse   the rhythm of the heart beating.

Pulse rate   how many times the heart beats in a minute.

Relax   when a muscle gets longer.

Reproduction/reproduce   making a new generation — animals have babies, new plants grow from seeds.

Respiration/respire   using oxygen to turn food into energy.

Ribs   the bones in the chest that protect the heart and lungs.

Root   the part of a plant under the ground that takes in water.

Sepal   protects the petals when the flower's still in the bud.

Side effect   something that happens as well as what was supposed to happen.

Skull   the bones that protect the brain.

Spine   the backbone.

Stamen   the male part of a flower.

Starches   a type of carbohydrate, e.g: pasta.

Stem   holds a plant upright.

Stigma   at the top of the carpel, where pollen lands.

Style   the bit that holds up the stigma.

Sugars   a type of carbohydrate, e.g: honey.

Tendon   joins muscle to bone.

Variation   differences in living things.

Vein   takes blood back to the heart.

Vertebrate   animal with a backbone.

Virus   a type of microbe.

SECTION FIVE — LIVING THINGS IN THEIR ENVIRONMENT

Natural or Man-Made

Everything in the world is made from *MATERIALS* — it's just stuff things are made of.

1) Some things are made of Natural Materials

a) Some *NATURAL MATERIALS* come from *UNDERGROUND*.

For example:

Oil

Rock

Precious metals and stones

Slate

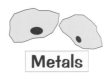
Metals

Clay

b) Some *NATURAL MATERIALS* come from *LIVING THINGS*.

For example:

Soft wood

Hard wood

Wool

cotton

Leather

Silk

rubber

2) Some things are made of Synthetic (Man-Made) Materials

For example:

Nylon/ polyester

Plastic

Fleece fabric

Fibreglass

Natural or Man-Made

3) Some things are made of Natural Materials

...which have been changed

For example:

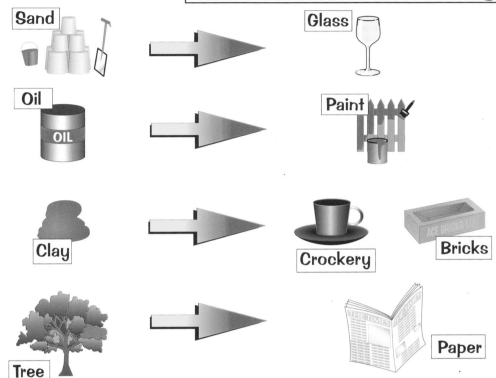

4) Some Materials have been Recycled

For example:

Old Newspapers

Toilet paper

5) Some Materials have been Combined

For example:

It's a material world and don't you forget it....

Don't forget that *materials* means the stuff that something's *made* from. It doesn't mean the same as fabric. We still call them materials whether they are natural or man-made. *Rubber's* actually from a *plant*, although it doesn't feel like something natural. Remember that materials can be combined to give a new material.

Comparing Materials

Materials have certain PROPERTIES which make them Useful

You need to be able to describe and compare the properties of a material and say why it's used for a job. We use certain materials for certain jobs...

1) Because they are _STRONG_ (Sturdy)

Steel bridge

Bleach — Plastic container

2) Because they are _HARD_ (Difficult to scratch)

Diamond cutter

Metal hammer head

3) Because they are _FLEXIBLE_ (Bendy)

fishing rod

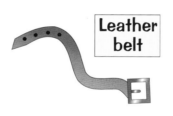

Leather belt

4) Because they are _RIGID_ (Stiff)

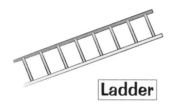

Ladder

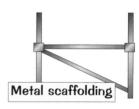

Metal scaffolding

5) Because they can be _MOULDED_ (Shaped)

Safety helmet

Metal coin

Glass bottle

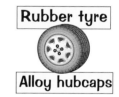

Rubber tyre

Alloy hubcaps

6) Because they are _ABSORBENT_ (Soaks up liquids)

Paper wadding

Towelling textile

7) Because they are _WATERPROOF_ (Repels liquids)

Canvas tent

Nylon umbrella

Comparing Materials

8) Because they are *TRANSPARENT* (See-through)

Glass

OR **9)** *OPAQUE* (Not see-through)

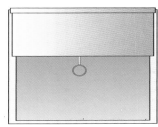

Fabric

10) Because they can *FLOAT* (Won't sink)

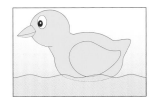

Plastic duck

OR **11)** *SINK* (Won't float)

Metal anchor

12) Because they can *STRETCH*

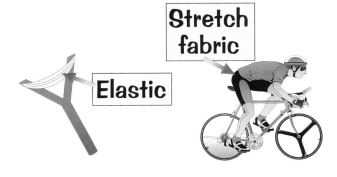

Stretch fabric

Elastic

OR **13)** be *COMPRESSED* (Squashed)

Metal spring

Be strong, be tough — learn all these words...

We choose to use certain materials for certain jobs because their special properties make them suitable. It'd be *no good* trying to dry yourself with a *plastic sheet*, or bang a nail in with a *cushion*, would it? Remember how you chose what paper was best for mopping up water spills by doing a *fair test*.

Conductors and Insulators of Heat

1) Some Materials let Heat Pass through them Easily

1) These materials are called *THERMAL CONDUCTORS*.
2) *METALS* are good *THERMAL CONDUCTORS*.
3) Because heat passes through them quickly
   — metals normally feel *COLD*.

2) Some Materials Do Not let Heat Pass through them

1) Materials that do not let heat pass through them are called *THERMAL INSULATORS*.

Plastic kettle **Cork pot stand** **Wooden handle** **Oven glove** **Thermal vest**

2) Plastic, cork, wood and fabrics are good *THERMAL INSULATORS*.
3) Thermal insulators are good for keeping heat *OUT* as well as *IN*.

HEAT OUT

Cool box
keep it cool

Thermos
DOES BOTH

HEAT IN
Polystyrene cup

keep it hot

A _GOOD INSULATOR_ = A _POOR CONDUCTOR_

3) Heat Travels from a Warmer Material to a Colder one

HOT   COLD

HEAT ➡

Heat is like a tourist — it loves to travel...

Remember that heat *only* moves from *hot* things to *colder* things, *never* the other way round. Some things let heat travel through them easily and others don't. Think of a saucepan — the heat goes through the *pan* to the food, but *not* through the *handle* to your fingers. Remember, the same material that keeps heat out of something can also keep heat in.

Conductors and Insulators of Electricity

1) Conductors Let Electricity Flow through them

1) Materials that can carry electricity are called *conductors* — they *conduct* electricity.
2) *Metals* like copper, iron, steel and aluminium are all good conductors.

2) Insulators do not let Electricity Flow through them

1) Materials that can *not* carry electricity are called *insulators* — they don't conduct electricity.
2) Wood, plastic, glass and rubber are all insulators.

Wood

Plastic

Glass

Rubber

3) Insulators and Conductors both have Important Uses

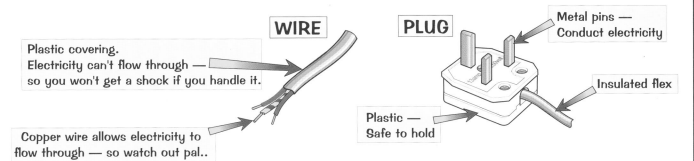

WIRE

PLUG

Plastic covering.
Electricity can't flow through —
so you won't get a shock if you handle it.

Copper wire allows electricity to
flow through — so watch out pal..

Metal pins —
Conduct electricity

Insulated flex

Plastic —
Safe to hold

4) Electricity can be dangerous

You shouldn't touch *anything* electrical with wet hands
— and that includes *switches*. Electricity can conducted
through sweat (salty water) to your body,
giving you an electric shock, and that's no joke.

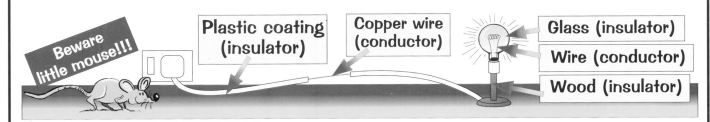

Beware
little mouse!!!

Plastic coating
(insulator)

Copper wire
(conductor)

Glass (insulator)

Wire (conductor)

Wood (insulator)

Learn about electricity — don't let it shock you...

You need to know which materials conduct electricity, and what materials are insulators.
Remember how you'd make a *circuit* to test materials to see if they conduct electricity. Don't
forget that mains electricity can be very *dangerous*, so learn those safety rules.

Magnetic Materials

1) Only Metals are Attracted to Magnets

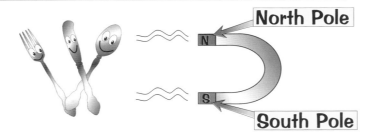

2) No Other Materials are Attracted to Magnets

Wood, plastic, glass and everything else are *not* attracted to magnets.

No chance matey

3) Not All Metals are Attracted to Magnets

IRON and STEEL = YES ✓

AlUMINIUM
BRASS and COPPER = No ✗

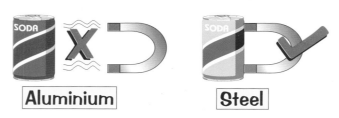

Aluminium   Steel

4) Some Magnets are Stronger than others

This bar magnet holds more paper clips than the horseshoe — so it's *stronger*.

Bar magnet

Strong

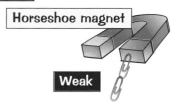

Horseshoe magnet

Weak

Feel attractive — you must be a magnet...

Magnetism is a bit weird when you think about it — a magnet can pick up paperclips without even touching them... Remember, *only* metals are magnetic, but *not all* metals are magnetic. You need to get the difference between being magnetic and actually being a magnet straight in your mind. Think about two magnets *repelling* each other — *only* magnets can do that.

Wood

1) Wood comes from Trees and is a Natural Material

1) Most hardwoods come from deciduous
(*loses its leaves*) trees.

2) Most softwoods come from
evergreen (*doesn't lose its leaves*) trees.

2) Wood has Many Useful Properties

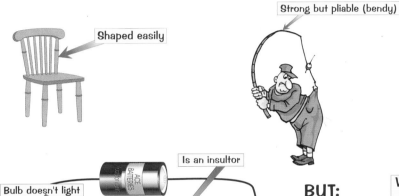

Shaped easily

Strong but pliable (bendy)

Floats

Is an insultor

Bulb doesn't light

BUT:

Wood needs protecting
or it will rot away

3) Changing Wood can make it more Useful

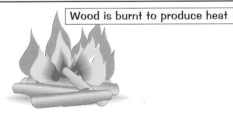

Wood is burnt to produce heat

Made into charcoal

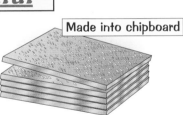

Made into chipboard

4) Wood is mashed up to make Paper

1) Paper is manufactured (*made*) from wood.

2) Some types of paper have
different properties — great
for different jobs.

3) Paper can be recycled and it can rot.

PAPER

Wood — it's better than bad, it's good....

Wood's so useful for so many things — that's because it's got lots of useful properties. If you keep on planting *new* trees to *replace* the ones you cut down, you *won't run out* of trees. Remember that *paper* is made from wood that's been all *chewed up*.

Plastics

1) Plastics are Synthetic Materials made from Oil

Plastics have plenty of *USEFUL PROPERTIES*.

1) They can be made to take on *any shape*.

2) They are *light* weight

3) They can be *coloured*, *opaque* or *transparent*.

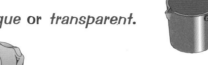

4) They are *strong*.

5) They are good *insulators*.

7) They are *waterproof*.

6) They are *nonmagnetic*.

2) Plastics are Difficult to get Rid Of

1) Some can be *reused* or *recycled*.

2) Most do not *rot*.

 40 years old and still going strong

 2 years old and nearly gone

3) Some new ones are *biodegradable* (will rot).

3) Plastics have Many Uses

 CLINGY FILM ACE PLASTIC SHOPPING BAG  ACE PAINT

Polythene   P.V.C.   Polyurethane   Polyester

Plastics — they're just ace...

Plastics can be made into loads of different things — just look at these pictures, would you.
Remember that there are lots of different sorts of plastic and their properties are all different.
Some of them can even be made into fabrics, like *nylon*.

Fabrics

1) **Fabrics are made up of Fibres Woven Together**

1) Some fibres are *natural*.

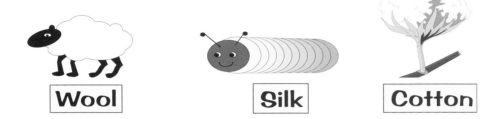

Wool   **Silk**   **Cotton**

2) Some fibres are *manmade*.

Polyester   **Nylon**

2) **Different Fabrics have Different Properties**

1) Denim is *hard-wearing*.

2) Silk is *light* and *cool*.

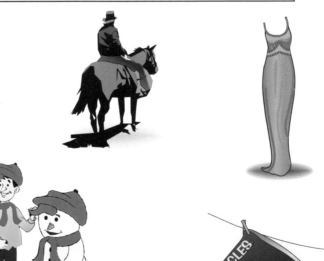

3) Wool is *warm*.

4) Nylon dries *easily*.

This page is good for you — it's got lots of fibre

The thing to remember is that you need *fibres* to make a *fabric*. They get spun into a thread which gets woven (or knitted) into fabric. Think about all the different clothes you wear and what they're made out of and if they're warm, cool, hard wearing or whatever.

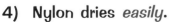

SECTION SIX — LOOKING AT MATERIALS

Glass

1) Glass is made from Heating Sand

Strange though it may sound!

2) Glass has many Useful Properties

Glass is transparent

Glass is strong but it can shatter

Glass can be moulded, or blown, or coloured

Glass can be used to make mirrors and lenses

SAY CHEESE!

Glass can be manufactured into glass fibre

3) Glass Does Not Rot

4) Glass can be Reused or Recycled

Empty bottles can be cleaned and used again, or crushed and melted to make new bottles.

Glass — it's just a smashing material...

Most glass is *transparent*, but some glass is patterned or made cloudy so that it's *translucent*. This means that light gets through but you can't see through it clearly. Use the diagrams to help you learn the four points about glass on this page.

Metals

1) Metals are Found Underground

1) Gold, silver and platinum are found as *pure lumps*.

2)

IRON,   **COPPER**,   **LEAD**,   **TIN**   and   **ALUMINIUM**
are all found *mixed in* with *rocks* (ores).

3) Some metals are *mixed* with other metals to make *new ones*.

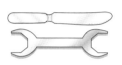

STEEL   **BRONZE**   **BRASS**

2) Metals have many useful properties

1) Metals are strong and tough

2) Metals are shiny

ACE SHINY TROPHY

3) Metals are easy to shape

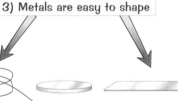

Pulled into wires   Moulded   Rolled into flat sheets

4) Metals make a noise when hit

DONG!

5) Metals can be reused and recycled

My car!?

6) Some metals are magnetic

7) Metals are good conductors of heat

8) Some metals are good conductors of electricity.

<u>BUT:</u> Metals *corrode* (rust).

Copper load at this lot...

There are loads of different types of metal. They all have quite a lot in common, though. Things made from metal are *hard*, and are usually *smooth* and *shiny*. Don't forget that metals originally come from the *ground*, usually mixed in with rocks.

Rocks

Rocks are all around — underground, on beaches, in gardens, buildings, walls, quarries, cemeteries. That's why they're dead useful and have been for yonks...

Not All rocks are the same

1) Some rocks are *HARDER*.

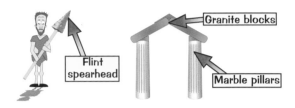

2) Some rocks are SOFTER.

4) Some rocks are *IMPERMEABLE*.

(They **DO NOT** allow water to **SOAK** through).

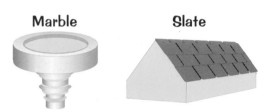

3) Some rocks are *PERMEABLE*.

(They allow water to **SOAK** through).

5) *CONGLOMERATE* rocks

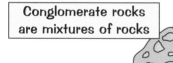
Conglomerate rocks are mixtures of rocks

6) *PEBBLES*

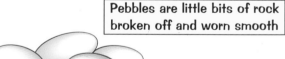
Pebbles are little bits of rock broken off and worn smooth

7) *FOSSILS*

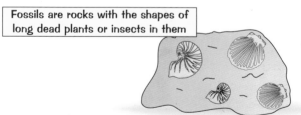
Fossils are rocks with the shapes of long dead plants or insects in them

Like it or lump it — you need to know about rocks...

There's plenty of words here to learn, and some of them do look a bit long and complicated. *Impermeable* means it's impossible for water to soak through. *Conglomerate* is just a collection of rocks all mixed up together.

Soil

1) We need Soil to Grow Plants for Food

Soil covers most of the world's land.

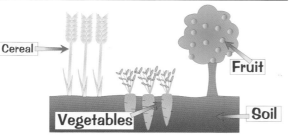

Cereal

Fruit

Vegetables

Soil

2) Soil is made from Four things

WORN DOWN ROCK + HUMUS + AIR + WATER

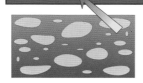

Humus is dead and rotting material.

3) Soil is Teeming with Life

Worms, insects, and termites eat, live and die in the soil.

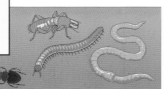

Bacteria

CHOMP!

CHOMP!

CHOMP!

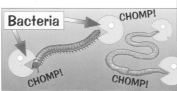

Microbes break down dead plants and animals.

4) Soils are Different because not all Rocks are the same

It depends what *kind* of *worn down rock* it comes from.

GRAVELLY SOIL
1) Full of small stones.
2) Water drains through quickly.

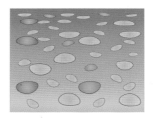

SANDY SOIL
1) Light and dry.
2) Air gaps so water drains through quickly.

CLAY SOIL
1) Very sticky when wet.
2) Heavy soil.
3) Water does not drain through quickly.

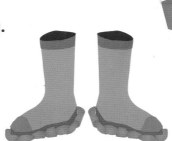

Soil — time to unearth the facts...

The really important thing here is to learn the four things that make up soil. Don't forget the *air* and *water* —they may not seem like much, but they're really important. Remember that different sorts of soil have different properties.

Solids, Liquids and Gases

All Materials can be put into Three Groups

BRICK

Metal spoon

SOLIDS

CHEESE

SOAP

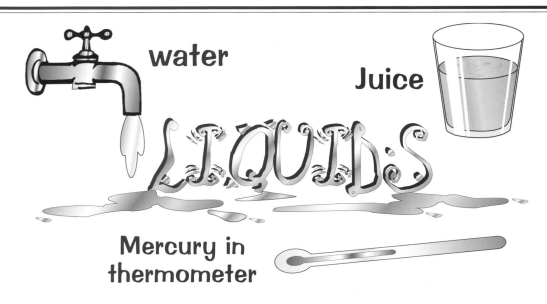

water

Juice

LIQUIDS

Mercury in thermometer

GASES

Properties of Solids, Liquids and Gases

 SOLIDS
.......are easy to control

2) Solids can be cut or shaped.

1) All the particles in solids are packed tightly together and can hardly move.

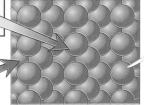

Help!! I'm getting squashed in here!!

2) Solids keep their shape.

3) Anything you can take hold of is solid.

 LIQUIDS
.......are more difficult to control
They keep wanting to run away!!

3) Liquids take up the shape of any container.

sook!!

1) The particles in liquids are not so tightly packed and can move a little.

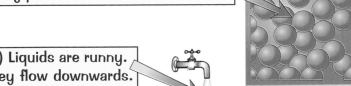

Excuse me!! Let me through!!

2) Liquids are runny. They flow downwards.

4) The surface of a liquid in a container stays level.

GASES
....are very hard to control.
They keep wanting to escape!!

3) Most gases are invisible.

1) The particles that make up gases have lots of room and move all over the place, all the time.

Wheeee!! This is great fun!!

2) Gases are all around us, spreading into any empty space.

4) You can even make your own gas.

BURP!! Pardon me!!

Solids, liquids and gases — three for the price of one...

It's important to *learn* all the little *details* on this page to make sure that you *really* know the difference between a solid, a liquid and a gas. It does seem odd to think of them all being made up of little tiny particles, but in the long run it'll actually help if you can see it that way.

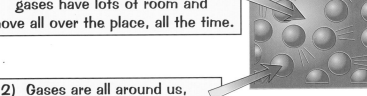

Summary Questions For Section Six

Try these. *Don't worry* if you get stuck. Look back but make sure you know them next time.

1) What do *materials* have which make them useful?
2) Why would *steel* be used to make a *bridge*?
3) Why is a tyre made of *rubber*?
4) Which material would be *best* to make a *toy boat*? Say *why*.
5) What things can you think of which have been *moulded*?
6) Finish this sentence: "Everything we use in the world is made _____".

7) Name *four* natural materials from *underground*.
8) What does *synthetic* mean?
9) What *new material* could be made from *clay*?
10) Name any *recycled* material.
11) Which is *true*: a) Heat can travel well through *all* materials; OR b) Heat can travel well through *some* materials?
12) What make good *thermal conductors*?

13) What is a *thermal insulator*?
14) Complete this sentence:
"Only _____ are attracted to magnets".
15) Would *electricity* be able to pass through:
a) Wood b) Metal c) Plastic?
16) What are the properties of *wood*?

17) Name some *advantages* and *disadvantages* of plastic.
18) What is *fabric* made up of?
19) How is nylon *different* from cotton?
20) Finish this:
"Transparency and strength are properties of _____".
21) Where are *metals* found?
22) How many *properties* of *metals* can you remember?

23) Name *five* metals. Can you remember even *more*?
24) Are all rocks the *same*? *Explain* your answer.
25) What is *soil* made up of?
26) What does *permeable* mean?
27) What are the *three groups* that materials fall into?
Solids, _____, _____.
28) What are *particles*?
29) I am *invisible*. I move *quickly* to fill any space. *What* am I?
30) Make up a similar sentence for *liquid*.

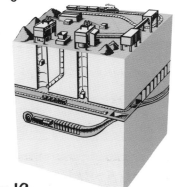

SECTION SIX — LOOKING AT MATERIALS

Mixing Materials

You can make mixtures of solids, liquids and gases

1)
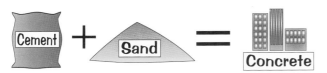

A mixture of SOLIDS

2)
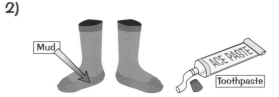

A mixture of SOLIDS+LIQUIDS

3)

smoke =
soot + air

A mixture of SOLIDS+GAS

4)

air + cream =
fluffy cream

air + juice =
fizzy pop

A mixture of GAS+LIQUIDS

Mixing with Water — a Solution

Some solids _dissolve_ when you _mix_ them with water. The new liquid is called a _solution_.

Sugar dissolves in _tea_. It changes into a sweet solution.

The _tablet_ dissolves in _water_. It changes into a funny tasting solution.

Gravy granules dissolve in _water_. They change into a solution of gravy.

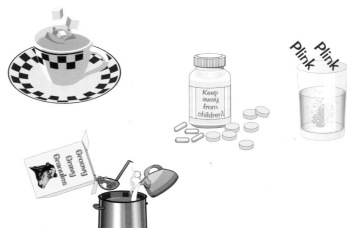

Dilute — means make less concentrated

1) You can _dilute_ liquids by adding water.

2) Orange squash is a _concentrated_ solution (you might say "strong").

3) Diluting — makes it _less_ concentrated (you might say "weaker").

Mixing materials — makes all the difference...

Solids, liquids and gases can all be mixed together, which is pretty _obvious_ if you think about it. Remember, when you dissolve a solid in a liquid, it doesn't disappear — it's still there. You'll find out about how to separate mixtures in Section Eight.

Physical Changes

Some Changes are Physical Changes

The materials do not break down but change how they look and feel. They make a *temporary* change. For example:

1) Chocolate *melts* (heat).

2) Water *freezes* (cold).

3) Water vapour *condenses* on a cold mirror (cold).

4) Puddles *evaporate* into air (heat).

Physical changes can be <u>reversed</u> (changed back)

Heating Materials can cause a Physical Change

Things Melt when you heat them and change how they look

For example SOLIDS change to a LIQUID.

chocolate

candle wax

when it *melts*, not when it burns.

butter

heater

Dangerous — so don't try this..

You could change them *back* if you cooled them. These changes can be <u>*REVERSED*</u>.

Physical Changes

Cooling Down Materials can cause Physical Changes

When you Cool a liquid it changes to a Solid

Changing from a liquid to a solid is called *freezing*.

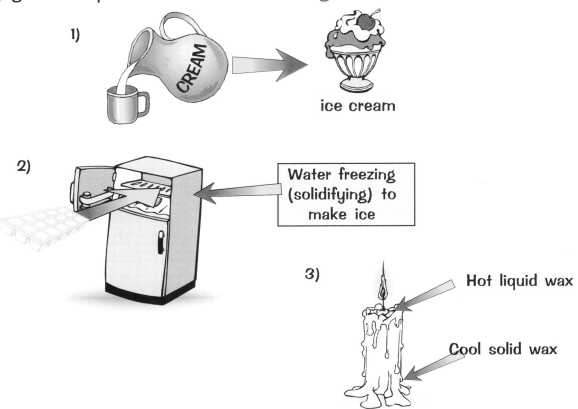

1) ice cream

2) Water freezing (solidifying) to make ice

3) Hot liquid wax

Cool solid wax

When you Cool soft solids they go Hard

Frozen chicken

You can *reverse* these changes by adding *HEAT*.

Physical Changes — they're a two way street...

You know that solids melt when they get hot enough, and then go back to solid when they're cooled back down — you've seen water *freezing* and ice *melting*. Don't forget, these changes *can* be *reversed*, the water isn't stuck as ice when it warms up again. Remember, solid, liquid and gas are the *states* that something's in and changes of state are called *physical changes*.

Chemical Changes

Some Changes are Chemical Changes

In a chemical change, the materials break down completely. They change completely into something else. This is a *permanent* change — it can't be reversed.

For example:

1) Wood and paper *burn* to ash.
2) Ingredients are *cooked*.
3) Dead plants and animals *decay* to humus.
4) Some metals *corrode* (rust).
5) Clay is *baked* into a pot.

Chemical changes cannot be Reversed

Some things cook when you heat them —

and change completely

Cooking is a chemical change because it's a permanent change. You can't get the ingredients back again once you've cooked them.

eggs + FLOUR = cake

+ MILK + heat

THIS CHANGE CANNOT BE REVERSED — you won't get the ingredients back out of the cake.

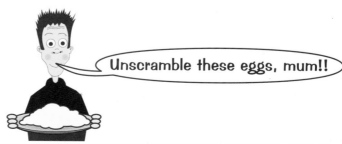

Unscramble these eggs, mum!!

Chemical Changes

Some things burn when you heat them

When materials are *burned* they *change completely*.
You *can't reverse* changes made by *burning*.

Burning Fuel — an Important Chemical Change

1) *Wood, coal* and *gas burn* to produce heat energy.

2) This can be converted *(changed)* into *electricity*.

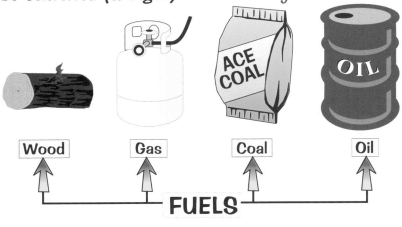

FUELS

3) They can produce *light* as well which is jolly.

4) *Fuels* can *burn* to drive machines like cars.

5) Our bodies *burn (use up)* food slowly to give us *energy*.

Food

ALL OF THESE CHANGES ARE CHEMICAL CHANGES — THEY CANNOT BE REVERSED

Chemical Changes — They're a one way street pal...

These are all changes that *can't* be undone. The chap at the bottom of the page there won't get his eggs unscrambled because it's impossible. Think about things that change when you add them to water, like plaster of Paris, which goes *dead hard* and sets. Don't forget that when something *burns* there's a *gas* given off that you can't see.

SECTION SEVEN — CHANGING MATERIALS

The Water Cycle

Temperature — How Hot and Cold

1) *Temperature* tells us how *hot* or *cold* things are.

2) We use a *thermometer* to measure *temperature*.

3) We measure *temperature* in *degrees celsius* — °C.

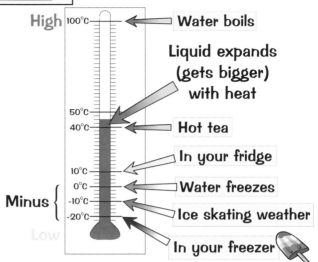

High   100°C ← Water boils

Liquid expands (gets bigger) with heat

50°C
40°C ← Hot tea

In your fridge

10°C
0°C ← Water freezes
Minus { -10°C ← Ice skating weather
-20°C

Low

In your freezer

Water has Three different Forms

The form *(or state)* that water takes depends on the temperature.

1) Solid Water — Ice

1) Water *freezes* at 0°C.

2) Water *expands* when it freezes.

3) Ice can *float*.

Water can be changed by cooling it

2) Liquid Water — Water!

1) Water is good for *dissolving* materials in.

2) Water has a tiny *surface* like a *skin* that some insects can walk on.

3) Water can be in the shape of *droplets*.

4) Water *vapour* is tiny droplets suspended in the air.

Water can be changed by heating it

3) Gaseous Water — Steam

1) Water *boils* (changes to steam) at 100°C.

2) Gaseous means — as a *gas*.

3) Steam is *invisible*.

4) Steam is very *dangerous*. It can burn you badly.

Steam

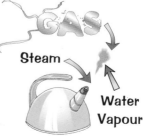

Water Vapour

The Water Cycle

This is the evaporation and condensation of water in the air. It keeps going all the time

Evaporation — turning to a gas

1) The sun can heat water. The water goes into the air
— it doesn't disappear. The water *evaporates* into a gas.

Puddle

2) The water from wet clothes
evaporates into the air.

**A LIQUID *EVAPORATES* INTO A GAS
WHEN IT IS *WARMED***

Condensation — turning from a gas back to a liquid

Cool mirror

Water droplets

Hot air

1) Water vapour in the air *cools* and
turns into water droplets.
2) The water vapour *condenses*.

**A GAS *CONDENSES* INTO A LIQUID
WHEN IT IS *COOLED***

Evaporation and Condensation of Water on Planet Earth

1) The water here on planet Earth is constantly recycling. Strange but true...
2) When the temperature gets really low rain drops can fall as snow or hail instead of rain.

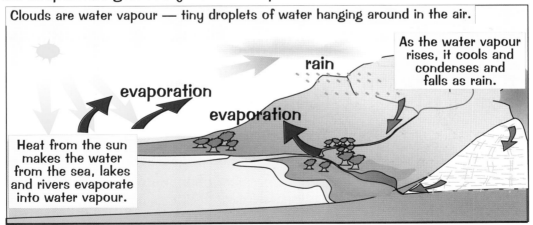

Clouds are water vapour — tiny droplets of water hanging around in the air.

As the water vapour rises, it cools and condenses and falls as rain.

rain

evaporation

evaporation

Heat from the sun makes the water from the sea, lakes and rivers evaporate into water vapour.

Water Cycle — sounds like a cross-channel bike..

Remember that ice, water and steam are all *states* of water. You really do need to know the words *evaporation* and *condensation*. Don't forget that water *doesn't* disappear when it evaporates, but it turns into a gas. Look at the diagram of the water cycle at the bottom of the page really carefully, and try to *follow* the water on its way around the picture.

Summary Questions For Section Seven

There are quite a lot of *long words* in this section that you'll be expected to use and understand. Don't let them put you off, they're all *explained* where they come up, and there's a *word list* at the end of section Eight that you'll find helpful. So, here are more lovely questions for you to try. You needn't do them all at once, but make sure you don't leave any out. The name of the game is to make sure that you can *do* them all, and then you'll know that you *understand* it all.

1) What happens to *sugar* when you *add* it to a cup of *tea*?
2) What is a *solution*?
3) What do you need to do to a *concentrated* solution to make it *weaker*?
4) What would happen if you added *oil* to *water*?
5) Explain what happens when you mix soil and *water*.
6) Complete this sentence:
   When you melt chocolate you are changing a solid to a _____.
7) Give an example of any change which *cannot* be *reversed*.
8) What happens to a *liquid* when you *freeze* it?
9) Finish this: A _____ tells you how *hot* or *cold* things are.
10) What *instrument* would you use to measure *temperature*?
11) At what temperature does:

   a) water *boil* b) water *freeze*?

   12) Is this true or false: "A cup of tea is at around -3°C".
      Explain what the "-" sign means before the "3" in -3°C.
   13) What *three* different forms does *water* have?
   14) Why is the top of a milk bottle forced off if the milk *freezes* on a cold day?
   15) Why does a pond skater insect *not sink*?
   16) What is *water vapour*?
   17) Why is *steam* so dangerous?
   18) Can you explain how *puddles* disappear?
   19) I want to get *salt crystals* from a solution of *salt* and *water*. How do I do it?
   20) True or false: A gas *evaporates* into a liquid when it is *cooled*.
      Explain your answer.
   21) The water on planet Earth recycles all the time.
      Explain this statement.

22) Choose the *correct* statement: a) *Physical* changes cannot be reversed;
                                      b) *Chemical* changes cannot be reversed.
23) Which of these are *physical* changes:
       water freezing; coal burning; ice cream melting; metal rusting.
24) What *chemical* change happens to dead plants and animals?
25) How many *different fuels* can you think of?
26) What has to happen to fuels so that they can produce heat and light *energy*?
27) Name the *fuel* the human *body* "burns".

SECTION SEVEN — CHANGING MATERIALS

Separating Mixtures of Materials

Separating mixed up materials can be pretty useful. In the kitchen, good cooks will separate the lumps from their flour when baking. Keen gardeners will separate stones from the soil of their seed beds and getting pure water is really important so we don't all get horribly ill.

Sieving — sorting out the Big Bits from the Small Bits

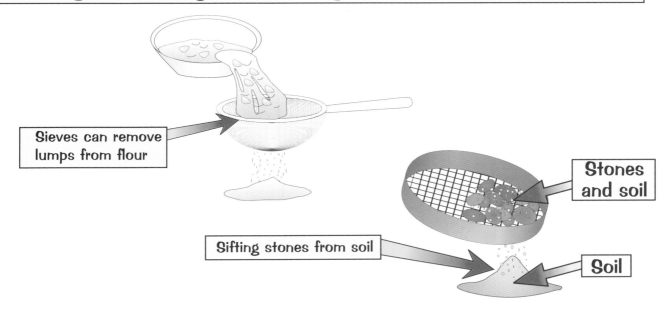

Sieves can remove lumps from flour

Stones and soil

Sifting stones from soil

Soil

Decanting — separating a Solid from a Liquid

In Ancient Egypt water was collected in large jars from the Nile. These would be left to stand to allow the mud, sand and silt to settle at the bottom of the jar.

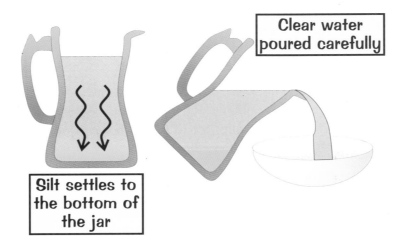

Clear water poured carefully

Silt settles to the bottom of the jar

Tipping the jar carefully allowed the solid (silt) and water to be separated...

...this is called, "Decanting".

Sieve through this page and pick out the important bits..

You've probably done this sort of thing in the classroom. Sieving something to separate the large bits from the small bits is pretty *easy*, but you need to know that decanting works because the mud and sand settle to the bottom.

Sorting Out a Mess

Filtering — separating Solid bits from a Liquid

A colander can separate peas from boiling water.

A tea strainer keeps the tea leaves out of the cup of tea.

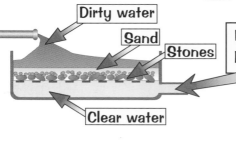

Dirty water

Sand

Stones

Clear water

Filter Beds are used to clean water. The dirty water is passed through a filter bed before it goes back to the river.

A home made filter bed can be made using different size stones, a pot and a jam jar.

Sand

Small Stones

Large Stones

Cloth

Jar

Filter paper can be used to separate very fine solids that are mixed with a liquid like water. The solids are not dissolved in the water and can't pass through the paper.

Evaporation — separating Soluble Solids from Water

Tea bag holds back large tea leaves

If the solids are small enough to pass through the filter paper with the water, you've got a problem. With tea, the tea leaves can't pass through the bag, but the brown flavouring is dissolved in the water and can pass through the filter (good for drinking the tea, only a problem when you want to separate the flavouring from the water) Follow the diagram to see what you do. Smashing fun.

(You can heat and evaporate off the water by using a flame, or just put the water and solid in a wide dish and leave it in a warm place.)

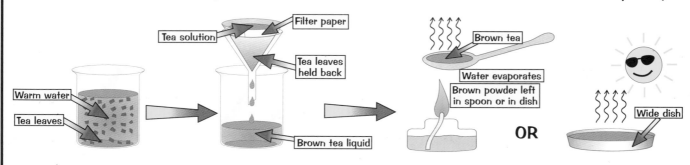

Warm water

Tea leaves

Tea solution

Filter paper

Tea leaves held back

Brown tea liquid

Brown tea

Water evaporates

Brown powder left in spoon or in dish

OR

Wide dish

Electricity

Get switched on to this — it's a powerful section.

1) **We get Electricity from the** Mains **or from** Batteries

1) Many *appliances (devices)* in our homes use mains electricity to work. Without it our lives would be *darker*, *duller* and *colder*.

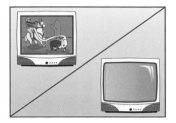
Television/Computers

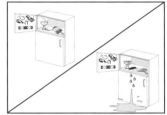
Fridge/Freezer

Lights

Heaters

2) Smaller electrical appliances often use *batteries* which store electricity. These appliances can be *moved* from place to place. Batteries eventually *run down* and need to be *replaced* or *re-charged*.

Clocks
Radios

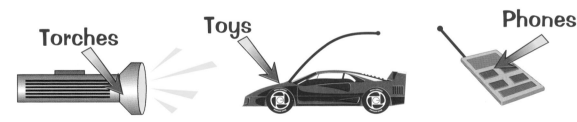
Torches
Toys
Phones

2) **Electricity can be** Dangerous

1) An electric shock from a mains socket *could kill you*. Electricity from the mains is a lot more powerful than electricity from a battery.

<u>NEVER</u> stick scissors, pens, fingers or anything else into a mains socket.
<u>NEVER</u> touch switches with wet hands.
<u>NEVER</u> use electrical appliances near water.
<u>ALWAYS</u> hold the plastic part of a plug when plugging in and unplugging appliances.

2) Re-chargeable batteries can discharge quickly and cause burns.

Safety Rules — deadly serious...

Remember, you need to be very careful when using electricity — the safety rules aren't just for the test, they're for everyday life. You need to know the difference between electricity from the *mains* and electricity from *batteries*.

Electric Circuits

1) Electricity can only Travel if there's a Complete Circuit

1) Electricity travels from the *power source*, such as a battery, round a series of *conductors* (*the circuit*) *back* to the power source.

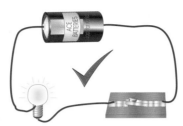

2) If there's a *gap* in the circuit — *no* electricity will flow.

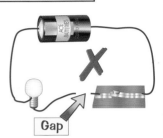

Gap

2) Simple Circuits can be set up using Components

Components are just things that can go in the circuit. An electrical circuit needs —

1) A *battery* or batteries, with wires connected to both the positive (+) and the negative (-) ends.

2) Wires made of *metal (of course)*.

3) An electrical *component (device)* such as a bulb, a buzzer or a motor.

3) The Batteries and Components must be set up Properly

Batteries and components must be put together correctly for the circuit to work.

The circuit A *won't work* because the wire has been connected to the glass on the bulb which is an insulator. ☹

A

Circuit B *won't work* because both wires are connected to the same end of the battery. ☹

B

Circuit C *won't work* because there is a gap in the circuit. ☹

C

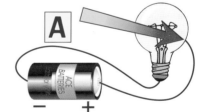
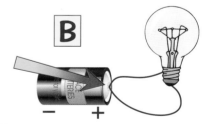

HOORAY! Circuit D *will work*. ☺
(as long as the battery isn't flat).

D

Electric Circuits

4) Circuit Diagrams use Symbols instead of Pictures

Make sure you know these symbols, and use them when you're drawing circuit diagrams:

Component	Picture	Symbol
Battery		—⊣⊢—
Two batteries		—⊣⊢⊣⊢—
Bulb		—⊗—or —○—
Buzzer		⏚
Motor		—Ⓜ—
Switch-off		—○ ╱ ○—
Switch-on		—○—○—

DRAW CIRCUIT DIAGRAMS ACCURATELY

———

There should not be gaps between wires and components.

A circuit diagram showing battery, wires, three switches, a bulb and a buzzer.

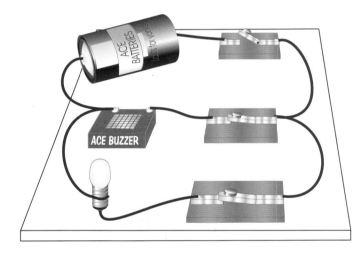

=

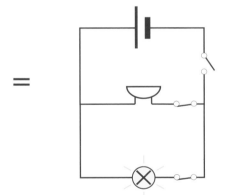

5) If there's no component in the circuit, there'll be a short-circuit

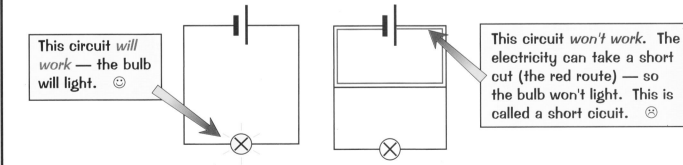

This circuit *will work* — the bulb will light. ☺

This circuit *won't work*. The electricity can take a short cut (the red route) — so the bulb won't light. This is called a short cicuit. ☹

Use symbols in circuits — but do it quietly...

This electricity stuff does look a bit complicated, but if you think back to the *investigations* you've done and remember the *basic facts* on these pages, you should be sorted. Electricity has to get from one end of the battery back to the other end of the battery for the circuit to work. Remember, *no* electricity will flow if there's a *gap* in the circuit. Circuit diagrams use symbols as a kind of shorthand, and yes, you *really do* need to *learn* all the symbols.

Changing Circuits

You know how to make a bulb light — well here's some more brill stuff you can do to control where the electricity goes and where it doesn't go.

1) *Switches* Control the Flow of Electricity in a Circuit

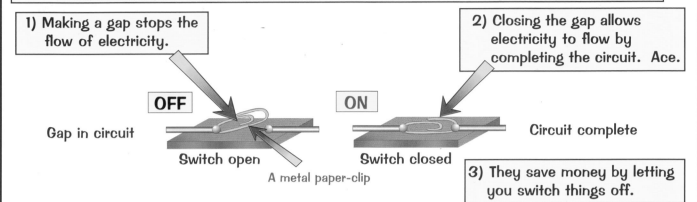

1) Making a gap stops the flow of electricity.

2) Closing the gap allows electricity to flow by completing the circuit. Ace.

OFF

Gap in circuit

Switch open

A metal paper-clip

ON

Switch closed

Circuit complete

3) They save money by letting you switch things off.

2) *Switches* — *Control Part of a Circuit and Save Money*

Take a look at the switches in these circuit diagrams — some are *open* and some are *closed*. See if you can work out which bulbs will *light*.
(Cos I'm a nice guy — I've given you the answers below.)

Switches ① ② and ③ are *open*
— no current will flow.
Bulb A or B will *NOT* light.

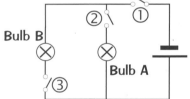

Switch ① is *open*
— so the electricity cannot flow around.
Bulb A or B will *NOT* light.

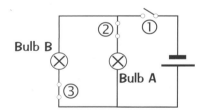

Switches ① and ② are *closed*
— so only bulb *A* lights. The *red* line shows the way the electricity flows.

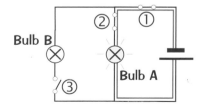

Switches ① and ③ are *closed*. This time only bulb *B* lights. The red line shows the route the electricity flows.

Remember if the bulb is off
— it saves you money.

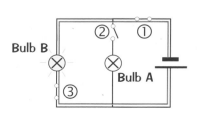

Changing Circuits

Now it's time to look at some very slightly more complicated circuits. (*don't panic*)

3) Altering Simple Circuits

Starting with a simple circuit — using a battery, switch, bulb and wire you can alter the number of batteries, the length of wire and the number of bulbs (but always alter one thing at a time).

Add More Batteries (in a line) — the bulb will be Brighter

In *"A LINE"* is known as *"IN SERIES"*

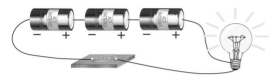
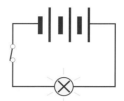

THE *MORE* BATTERIES — THE *BRIGHTER* THE BULB

TAKE CARE THOUGH — TOO MANY BATTERIES WILL DESTROY ("BLOW") THE BULB.

Add More Bulbs (in a line) — the bulbs will get Dimmer

The bulbs will be dimmer (*less bright*) than a single bulb would be in the same circuit.

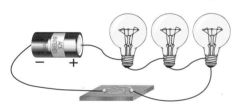
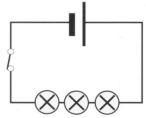

If we had three motors here instead, they'd turn slower than just one.

THE *MORE* BULBS — THE *FAINTER* THE LIGHT

The Longer the Wires — the Dimmer the Bulb

Long length of wire — bulb dim

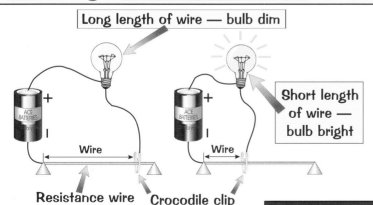

Short length of wire — bulb bright

Wire

Resistance wire   Crocodile clip

With normal wire, the effect is small. If you use a special type of wire called *resistance wire*, the brightness of the bulb will be reduced big time as you use longer wire.

THE *LONGER* THE WIRE — THE *FAINTER* THE BULB

Switch on your mind — but don't race around these circuits...

This stuff looks a bit more complicated, but if you think about it one step at a time then you'll get there. Remember electricity *can't flow* if there's a *gap* — that'll help you work out what bulbs will light in circuits with *switches*. The *more bulbs* you have in a circuit the *dimmer* they'll all be. And don't forget, the one nearest the battery is *not* brighter — they're all the same.

Summary Questions For Section Nine

Electricity may seem like a tough topic but it's not nearly as bad as it looks. It's the circuit diagrams that make it seem frightening — but *remember* the diagrams are just an *easier* way to draw a *picture* of the real circuit. *Practise* drawing circuit diagrams containing *switches*, *batteries* and different *components*.

Remember that the idea is to keep on bashing away at these questions until you can do *all* of them. If one or two look a bit tricky, *don't* leave them out, but go back and look through the section again, and keep trying. And don't forget to smile...

1) Name *four* things that would not work in your house if there was no electricity.
2) Why is it better for some appliances to work from *batteries*?
3) Why must you *not* push things (*other than plugs*) into mains sockets?
4) *Why* should you *not touch* a mains switch or plug with *wet* hands?
5) Why do *bathroom* light switches often have a cord hanging from them?
6) Why do you need a *metal* on the inside of a wire?
7) Why is there usually a *plastic coating* around a metal wire?
8) Why do people often wear *rubber* gloves and boots when using electrical garden tools?
9) What happens when a circuit has a break (or gap) in it?
10) Should you connect *both* ends of a battery into a circuit?
11) Name three electrical components used in simple circuits.
12) Imagine you have made a simple circuit using a battery, two wires and a bulb. The bulb doesn't light up. Give *three* reasons to explain what might be wrong.
13) What will happen if you try to complete a circuit by joining the glass of a light bulb to the battery? Explain this.
14) Draw a *circuit diagram* showing a circuit with:
     a battery, wires, an open switch and a bulb.
15) Draw a *circuit diagram* showing a circuit with:
     two batteries, wires, an open switch and a buzzer.
16) When do you get a *short-circuit*?
17) How does a simple *switch* work?

18) Is the switch opposite: a) ON or b) OFF?
19) Draw a circuit diagram to show how *switches* can be used to control two different parts of a circuit.
20) If you add an *extra* battery to a circuit containing a bulb, *how* will this affect the bulb?
21) What might happen to the bulb if you added *too many* extra batteries to the circuit?
22) How would you make a bulb in a circuit shine with a *fainter* light? Suggest *two* ways to do this.

Forces

I can't force you to learn any of this ...

1) A Force is either a Push or a Pull

Forces can make things:

1) SPEED UP

2) SLOW DOWN

3) CHANGE DIRECTION

4) CHANGE SHAPE

By Gum!!
Look at the
stretch on that!!

2) Forces are measured in newtons (N)

Forces are often measured using a spring-balance
called a force meter (or newton meter).

A spring-balance

3) Arrows Show Direction and Size of a Force

If two forces push or pull against each other and one is bigger than the other
— the *bigger one wins*.

Big Force   Small Force

Big force acting
to the RIGHT

Small force acting
to the LEFT

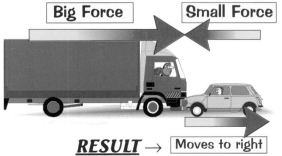

RESULT →   Moves to right

You can't see Forces — honest, I'm not pulling your leg...

Pretty straightforward stuff this. Don't forget that you *can't see forces*, but you can see the
effects of a force — something speeding up, slowing down, changing direction or changing
shape. You'll have had some practice *measuring* forces with a newton meter and *comparing*
different forces, so have a think back over your investigations to get your brain back in gear.

The Force of Friction and Air Resistance

Friction occurs when Two Surfaces Touch each other

1) Rougher surfaces slow things down a lot

Roads are rough to help you slow down quickly.

Screeeech

2) Smooth surfaces don't slow you down as much

Wheeeee!!!

Sometimes we want as little grip as possible.

3) Friction gives us grip

Without grip, starting and stopping is hard. That's why the soles of your trainers are such works of art.

4) Friction produces heat

That's why, when you rub your hands together, they get warm.

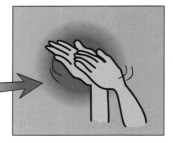

Air Resistance Slows Down Moving Objects

1) Air slows you down as you move through it — just like trying to wade through *deep water* — only not nearly so bad.

Not streamlined

Air resistance
Gravity
Slow down

2) To travel faster through air, things need to be *streamlined*.

3) To travel slower through air, you need a large *surface area* (like a parachute).

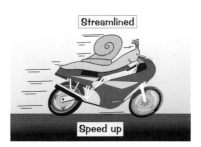
Streamlined
Speed up

Go on — Force yourself to get to grips with this section...

Friction acts when things touch and *air resistance* kinda slows you down when you move. Think about how easy or hard it is to *slide* on different surfaces. Don't forget, even though friction tends to slow things down it can be pretty *useful*. If there wasn't any friction everything would just slide out of your hands. Remember that the *bigger* the *area* you've got, the *more* air resistance you'll feel.

The Force of Gravity

You've learnt about two exciting forces with fancy names on the last page — now here's another one for you to learn — gravity.

Gravity pulls objects down towards the Centre of the Earth

1) Gravity pulls you down whether you're in the air, in water, or stood on the ground.

"What goes up, must come down".

2) The size of the gravitational force is pretty much the same all over the Earth. You would have to be a very, very long way from the Earth before you no longer felt the effect of its gravitational pull.

Free at last!!!

Three Great Ways to Beat Gravity

1) Exert a force in the *opposite direction*.

The bird's wings pushing against the air provide an upward force.

Gravity

2) Support yourself on a strong object — but make sure it's strong enough.

The car provides an *upward force* but, — in this case, not quite enough.

Gravity
Reaction force

3) In water, if the *upthrust* (see P. 82) matches the pull of gravity you will stay afloat.

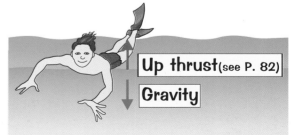

Up thrust (see P. 82)
Gravity

Gravity — very down-to-earth...

Remember that gravity pulls us towards the centre of the Earth, so it keeps us stuck on the Earth's surface. On the Moon, you feel the *Moon's gravity* rather than the Earth's. The Moon is *smaller* than the Earth, so the force of gravity is *less* and you don't get pulled down as much. The bottom part of the page is all about *balancing* the force of gravity so you *don't* keep on falling — more on balancing forces coming right up...

Upthrust is a Force

Upthrust is the Force Pushing Up on an Object in Water (or Air)

You've probably seen that things weigh less when they're held in water. This is because the water *pushes up* and *cancels out* some of the force of *gravity* pulling down.

1) Upthrust is much *greater* in *water* than in *air*.

2) The *size* of the upthrust in water depends on *how much* water has been pushed out of the way by the object. A large object pushes away loads of water so the upthrust is big.

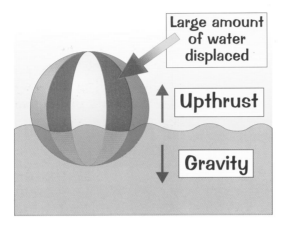

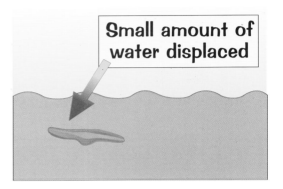

Gravity *equals* upthrust so the ball floats. The forces are *balanced*, so there's no movement.

The deflated beach ball sinks because now the *upthrust* is *smaller*, and *less* than gravity.

Learn this

> When the upthrust is *EQUAL* to the force of *GRAVITY*, an object will *FLOAT* because the two forces are *BALANCED*

WATCH OUT!

Don't fall into the trap of thinking that just because an object is *big* that it will necessarily float *better*. After all — which would you rather have on your foot — a bucket of *concrete* or a bucket of *polystyrene*. (no prizes for saying the polystyrene).
We say the *concrete* is more *dense* — it's a lot *heavier* for its size. Because it's a lot heavier, the force of gravity pulling it down is a lot more. That's why the concrete *sinks* and the polystyrene *floats* — even though the buckets are the same size.

Gravity won't get you down — if you've got support ...

This is really really *important* — things don't stay in place because gravity has got less but because there is *another force* acting in the opposite direction. Don't go writing anything like "it floats because gravity doesn't go through water" either, because that'd be *dead wrong*.

Balanced Forces

When Forces are Balanced — things don't start to move

1) The boat floats because the *upthrust* (upward force) is *equal* to *gravity* (the downward force).

upthrust

Gravity

2) No-one's going anywhere here because the force of the donkey pulling *one* way *equals* the force of the man pulling the *other* way.

Man pulling ⬅️ ➡️ Stubborn Donkey pulling

3) The balloon is suspended in the air when the *upthrust* from the air *equals* the pull of *gravity*.

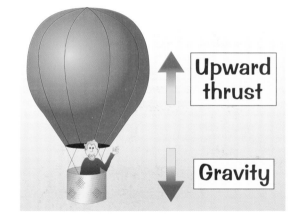

Upward thrust

Gravity

4) The weight of the table is pulled down by *gravity*, but the floor balances this and pushes *upwards* (*we say it provides an upthrust*) so the table does not move. Ace.

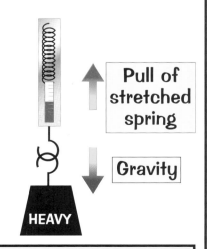

Pull of stretched spring

Gravity

HEAVY

5) The weight is suspended because the *pull* of the spring *equals* (*is balanced by*) the downward pull of *gravity* on the weight.

Balanced forces — they're still not moving me...

The point to remember here is that just because something's still it *doesn't* mean there are *no* forces acting on it. When two forces are *balanced*, they *cancel out* so the thing doesn't move. Have a go at drawing the diagrams on this page with the forces marked in and named.

Unbalanced Forces

When Forces are Unbalanced, things get Moving

1) Gravity is *greater* than the *upthrust* so the boat moves and unfortunately sinks.

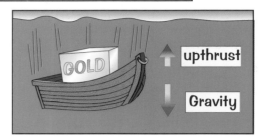

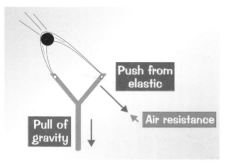

2) The *push* from the elastic is *greater* than the *air resistance* or *gravity* so the missile shoots away.

3) I don't know who this bloke thinks he is, but he's heading for trouble. The force of *gravity* is much *greater* than *air resistance* or his *upthrust*. Oops...

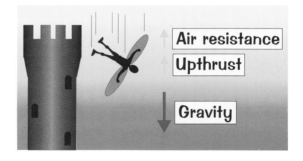

Magnets exert a force on other Magnets or Magnetic Materials

1) A north and a south pole *attract* each other.

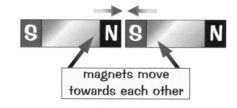

magnets move towards each other

2) *Two* north poles *repel* each other.

magnets move away from each other

3) *Two* south poles *repel* each other.

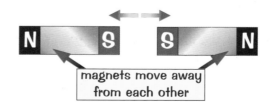

magnets move away from each other

More forces — to attract you to this...

If the forces on something still are balanced, the forces on something moving must be... well it's not quite as simple as that, unfortunately. Remember, forces make things *speed up* or *slow down* and they *start* or *stop* things moving. Moving at a *constant* speed means *balanced* forces.

Summary Questions For Section Ten

Well, here it is, the page you've all been waiting for. This is where you'll find out just how well you *know* your *forces*. Some of these questions may *stretch* you a bit... You'll have to be able to apply what you know about forces to lots of different situations. You'll definitely need to know these forces: friction, air resistance, gravity and upthrust. It's a good idea to be able to spell them too, so that the exam marker will know what you're talking about.

1) What *two* ways do forces work?
2) What are the *four* things that forces can *cause* objects to do?
3) What are the *units* of force?
4) What *instrument* would you use to measure force?
5) What is *friction*?
6) What sort of *surface* should a *slide* have so that you could go down it really fast?
7) What is the *name* of the force that gives us *grip*?
8) Why do we have good *grips* on our shoes?
9) What sort of *surface* should a slope have to *prevent* slipping?
10) What will be made when two surfaces *rub together*?
11) What is *air resistance*?
12) What *shape* should an object be in order to travel *faster* through the air?
13) Name something that needs to travel *slowly* through air. *How* does it manage this?
14) What is the *name* of the force that pulls objects *down* towards the centre of the Earth? Is there anywhere on Earth where you *don't* feel the effect of this force?

15) How do birds *overcome* the force of gravity and stay up in the air?
16) To stop a table in your classroom falling through the floor, what must the *floor* do against the force of gravity pulling the table down?
17) What *two* forces are acting on an object *floating* in water? Draw a diagram and show the forces on it.
18) What does the word *"upthrust"* mean?
19) If you use some plasticine to make a large *boat* shape, it will *float*, but if you use the same amount of plasticine to make a small round *ball*, it will *sink*. *Why* is this?
20) In terms of the *forces* acting upon it, why does a boat float?
21) What *two* forces are acting on a helium balloon floating in air?
22) In a tug-of-war, if both teams are pulling with *equal* force, what will happen?
23) Why is it dangerous to jump off a tall building? Explain this in terms of the forces acting on you...
24) When do two magnets *repel* one another?
25) When do two magnets *attract* one another?
26) Draw arrows to show the forces acting on the paper clips in the diagram opposite.

Sources of Light

If you're feeling in the dark about light and how you see then read on and all will be revealed.

1) Light Sources — Give Out Light

Light sources include: —

1) The Sun

2) Stars

3) Candle flame

4) Electric light

Some objects seem bright, but they are only *reflecting* light from elsewhere.
These are *NOT* light sources. These things include the moon, planets, mirrors and shiny objects.

Remember:

Light source   Not light sources...

2) Light has Three Important Properties

1) Light travels in *straight lines* from a light source to your eyes.

2) If something is in the way you get a *shadow*. (See P. 88)

3) Light travels *very fast*.

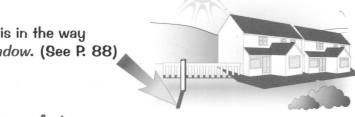

300,000,000 METRES EVERY SECOND

(That's 186,000 miles per second — That's fast).

How We See

We See things when Light from a Source Enters our Eyes

1) Light may come *directly* from the source to your eyes — like when you look at a *candle*.

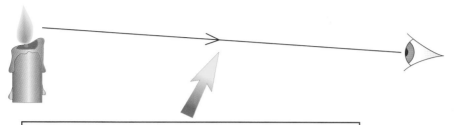

Put the arrow on the light ray *(light beam)* pointing away from the source and towards the eye.

2) Light also *bounces off* objects into your eyes — like when you look at a *cake*.

Wow! looks nice

When Light Bounces off Some Materials Better than Others

1) *Mirrors* and *shiny* objects reflect light well. Light bounces off the surface and into your eyes.

Mirror, Mirror on the wall, who's the fairest of them all?

YUK!

2) *Dull*, *dark* and *black* objects *don't* reflect light well. Light *can't* bounce off the surface.

Now do you see...

Remember, draw your light rays *straight* and make sure they start and finish *on* (not just near) the important objects. They go from the source to the eye, not the other way round. Learn your *light sources*, and remember that things like the Moon just *reflect* the Sun's light.

Shadows

Light can Pass Through some Materials

1) Materials that light can pass through are called *transparent*. Transparent materials include glass, clear plastic, water.

2) Materials that some light can pass through, but you can't see through clearly are called *translucent* — for example, a sandwich box or tissue paper.

3) Materials that light can't pass through are called *opaque*. Opaque materials include wood, metal, stone, next-door's cat and you.

When light from a Source is Blocked — you get a Shadow

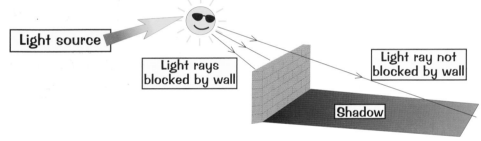

1) The more directly *overhead* the light source *(the sun)* is, the *shorter* the shadow.

2) The *closer* the light source to the object the *larger* the shadow.

Transparent — this page is as clear as day...

The words *transparent, opaque* and *translucent* have already popped up in the section about materials. Here's another chance to use them and learn what they mean. Have a look at the shadow diagrams and *follow* what's happening to the *rays of light* in each one.

Mirrors

Mirrors Reflect light Back at the same Angle

Light rays | Reflected light rays

1) If you put a mirror in the *right place*, you can even see round corners. Look at the rays of light in the diagram below.

Mum's happy — she thinks Tom is learning Science *but* — view this happy scene from above.

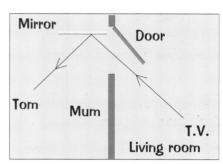

Scene from above.

Tom can see a fabulous program on TV, and thanks to the fact that light from the TV is reflected back at the same angle, Mum can't see it, so she doesn't suspect a thing....

2) Periscopes use a *pair* of mirrors to allow you to see round an object easily.

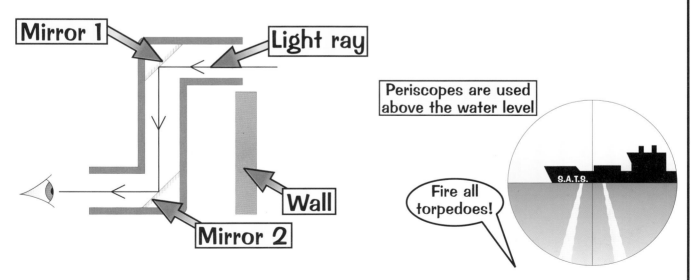

Mirrors — they'll help you reflect on this...

You can see that when light hits a mirror it bounces back off, and you get a *reflection*. If you use a mirror, you can see behind you or even round a corner. Follow the *light rays* in the diagrams if you're not sure. Also, don't forget the important rule — a light ray hitting a mirror is reflected back at the same angle.

Making Sound

Here's all you'll need to know about sound — in just two pages. Sounds too good to be true...

1) Sound happens when Something _Vibrates_

1) It may be obvious what is vibrating, and making the noise.

2) Or — it may not. Here it's the air in the bottle which is vibrating to produce the noise.

2) Sounds are _Transmitted_ through _Air_ or _Another Material_

1) Vibrating objects make the air or material next to it vibrate as well. So the vibrations kind of travel (are transmitted) through the air.

2) Sound can travel through all kinds of materials — like stone, brick, water and glass.

3) Sound cannot travel through a vacuum — because there is nothing to vibrate.

3) _We hear sounds when the_ _Vibrating Air_ _hits our_ _Ear Drums_

1) The _vibrating air_ (or material) hits our _ear drums_ and makes them vibrate.

2) This vibration is picked up by our _brains_.

OBJECT VIBRATES → AIR VIBRATES → EAR DRUM VIBRATES

Changing Sound

The More Energy in the Vibration — the LOUDER the Sound

That just means the *harder* you hit something, the *louder* the noise.

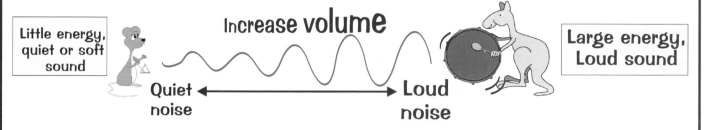

| Little energy, quiet or soft sound |
| Large energy, Loud sound |

Increase volume

Quiet noise ← → Loud noise

BUT — don't test this rule on your little brother — it will work, but Mum won't like it.

The Pitch is how High or Low a Note is

1) The *shorter* the vibrating object, the *higher* pitched the note.

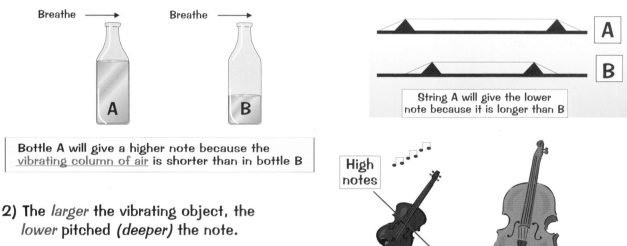

Breathe → A   Breathe → B

Bottle A will give a higher note because the <u>vibrating column of air</u> is shorter than in bottle B

String A will give the lower note because it is longer than B

High notes

2) The *larger* the vibrating object, the *lower* pitched *(deeper)* the note.

Low notes

The Tighter the String, the Higher the Pitch of the Note

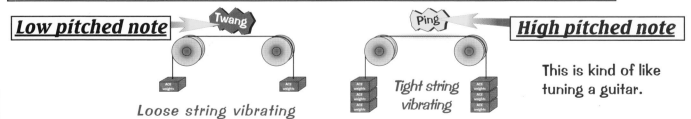

Low pitched note   Twang   Ping   **High pitched note**

Loose string vibrating   Tight string vibrating

This is kind of like tuning a guitar.

Now it's your turn to pitch in — and learn this lot...

As you may have noticed — *vibration* and *vibrating* are the in words on this page, so learn them. Make sure you know *what's* vibrating to make the sound, and you need to remember that for you to hear a sound, the *air* has to vibrate and then your *eardrum* has to vibrate. Thinking about musical instruments or elastic bands will help you remember about *pitch*.

Summary Questions For Section Eleven

Right then, you reckon you've learnt the last few pages about light and sound. Now for the *moment of truth*. Work your merry way through these questions until you can do them *all* with no worries. If you do get stuck, look back in the text for the answers — it's all there.
If you draw a diagram with rays in, use a ruler for the rays, and don't forget to put arrows on the rays pointing in the right direction.

1) Which of the following are *sources* of light?

Candle   Moon   Torch   Sun   Silver foil.
a)   b)   c)   d)   e)

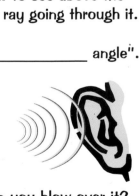

2) Explain *why* light shines off a silver brooch in bright sunlight.
3) Which of the following statements is true, a) or b)?
    a) We see an object when light from our eyes hits that object.
    b) We see an object when light from that object hits our eyes.
4) Draw a diagram *(with light rays)* to show how we see a tree on a sunny day.
5) How are *shadows* formed?
6) How could you make a *really large* shadow of your hand appear on a screen?
7) Finish this sentence about the size of shadows: "The *further* the source of light is from an object, the _____ the _____".
8) On a sunny day, at what *time* of day will your shadow be *shortest*?
9) What does the word "*opaque*" mean? Give an *example* of an opaque material.
10) What does the word "*translucent*" mean? Give an *example* of something translucent.
11) What does the word "*transparent*" mean? Give an *example* of a transparent material.
12) Explain why you can see yourself when you look in a mirror.
13) What sort of objects *reflect* light well?
14) What sort of objects do not reflect light well?
15) Draw a diagram to show how a light ray hitting a mirror at an angle bounces off.
16) What's the name of the instrument used in a submarine to allow the crew to see above the surface of the water? Sketch a diagram of this instrument, showing a light ray going through it.
17) Complete this sentence:
  "A light ray hitting a mirror at an angle is reflected off at_____ _____ angle".
18) How are *sounds* produced?
19) Name *five* things that sound can travel through.
20) Name *one* thing that sound can't travel through and explain why not.
21) How do we hear sounds? *(don't just say with our ears — give details)*.
22) Which is higher pitched, a *large* recorder or a *small* one?
23) What is the *pitch* of a note?
24) Why does a bottle that is almost full of water produce a high note when you blow over it?
25) Tim decides that, as his teacher is looking the wrong way, he will produce a sound by twanging his ruler which is sticking over of the edge of his desk. How can he make:
    1) A really *loud* sound.
    2) A very *low pitched* sound.
26) *How* could you make the stretched skin on a drum give out a *higher* note?

SECTION ELEVEN — LIGHT AND SOUND

THE EARTH AND BEYOND

93

The Solar System

Science is not just about what's on or in the Earth, it's also about all that stuff up in space.

The Sun is a Star at the Centre of our Solar System

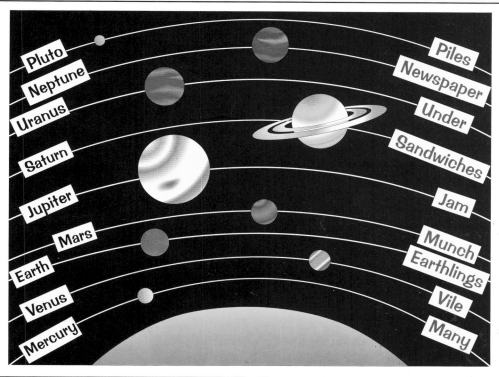

Pluto, Neptune, Uranus, Saturn, Jupiter, Mars, Earth, Venus, Mercury

Piles, Newspaper, Under, Sandwiches, Jam, Munch, Earthlings, Vile, Many

Seven Smart Facts about our Solar System

1) The Solar System consists of *all* the planets, asteroids and comets that *orbit* our Sun.

2) An orbit is the *path* an object takes through space around another object.

3) The planets are held in their orbits around the Sun by the Sun's *gravitational pull*.

4) The Sun, Earth, our Moon and the planets are roughly *spherical (round)*.

5) The Earth is the *third* planet from the Sun. Mercury and Venus are *closer* to the Sun than the Earth.

6) Mars, Jupiter, Saturn, Uranus, Neptune and Pluto are *further away*.

7) Use this handy "jollyism" to remember the *order* of the planets:—

Mercury	Venus	Earth	Mars	Jupiter	Saturn	Uranus	Neptune	Pluto
Many	Vile	Earthlings	Munch	Jam	Sandwiches	Under	Newspaper	Piles

The Solar System — it's out of this world man...

Right then, *seven* smart facts to be learnt and *one* smart diagram to help you remember it all. Remember that the Earth and the Sun are round. Think of some evidence you might have found that shows this.

SECTION TWELVE — THE EARTH AND BEYOND

The Moon

The Moon orbits the Earth

1) It takes about *28 days* for the Moon to orbit the Earth.

2) The Moon is held in its orbit round the Earth by the Earth's *gravitational pull*.

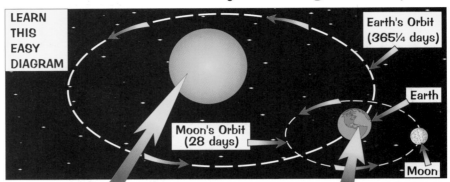

LEARN THIS EASY DIAGRAM

Earth's Orbit (365¼ days)

Earth

Moon's Orbit (28 days)

Moon

The Sun is bigger than the Earth, so its gravitational pull is larger than the Earth's.

The Earth is bigger than the Moon, so its gravitational pull is larger than the Moon's — that's why astronauts can jump higher on the Moon than on the Earth.

The Moon Appears to change Shape as it orbits the Earth

This is because we cannot always see the side of the Moon that's in sunlight **OR** we can only see part of the sunlit side of the Moon as it orbits the Earth.

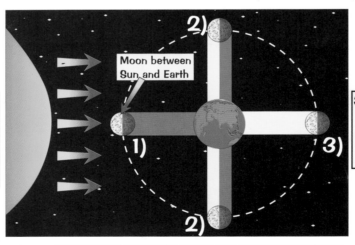

2)

Moon between Sun and Earth

1)

3)

2)

1) The dark side of the Moon is facing the Earth so we cannot see it — this is the *New Moon*.

3) We can see all the sunlit side of the Moon — this is the *Full Moon*.

2) We can see part of the Moon — the sunlit side — this is the *Half Moon*.

It's not fair!!

One side of the Moon is always in darkness. We cannot see the dark side of the Moon from Earth.

If you think you're just going round in circles —

I agree, there is quite a lot to learn on this page, but these are all the facts you'll need to know. If you learn this lot then you'll have got the Moon all sorted. Remember *what's* orbiting what, and how *long* it takes.

All in a Day

The movement of the Earth in space gives us day and night — here's how:

1) The Earth Rotates (spins) on its own Axis

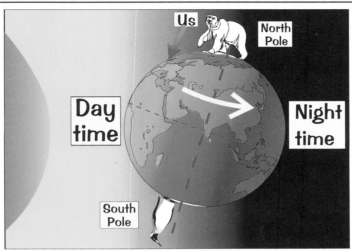

1) The Earth is *spherical (round)* and its *axis* is an imaginary line drawn through the centre of the Earth from the North Pole to the South Pole.

2) The Earth takes *24 hours* to completely rotate *(spin)* on its axis. *(24 hours = 1 day)*.

3) The side of the Earth *facing* the Sun is lit up — it's *daytime* for this side.

4) The side of the Earth facing *away* from the Sun is in darkness — it's *night-time* for this side.

5) The Earth's axis is slightly *tilted*.

The Sun doesn't Move — it's Us that Move

Because the Earth is moving, the Sun appears to move across the sky during as the day goes on.

Shadows are long in the morning and evening because the Sun is at its lowest in the sky.

Shadows are short at midday (noon) because the Sun is at its highest in the sky.

Remember — it's not your head that's spinning....it's the Earth

I know people always talk about the Sun rising and setting as if it's the Sun that goes round the Earth, but it's *not*, it's the other way around. It's a lot easier to understand all this if you've seen your teacher pretending that this torch is the Sun and this globe is the Earth (or whatever) and *spinning* the globe to get *day and night*. Entertainment indeed...

SECTION TWELVE — THE EARTH AND BEYOND

96

A Year

The Earth takes one Year to Orbit the Sun

1) It takes *365¼ days (one year)* for the Earth to *orbit* the Sun.

2) The Earth is held in its orbit round the Sun by the Sun's *gravity (gravitational pull)*.

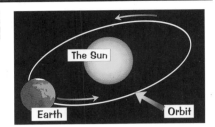

The Earth orbits the Sun on its tilted Axis giving us Seasons

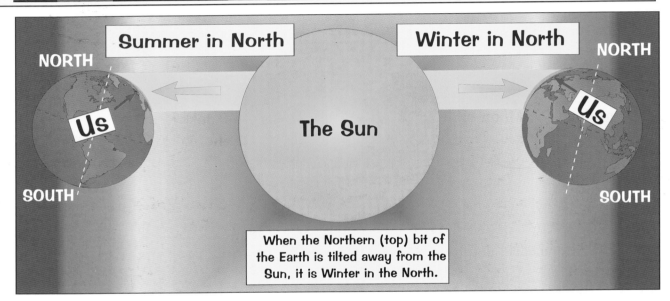

When the Northern (top) bit of the Earth is tilted away from the Sun, it is Winter in the North.

The Height of the Sun in the Sky Varies with the Seasons

1) The sun at *12.00pm* (noon) is highest in the sky on any given day.

2) But the sun is higher in *summer* than it is in the other three seasons.

3) This affects the length of *shadows* — the higher the sun, the shorter the shadow. (See P. 88)

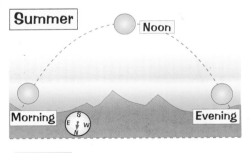

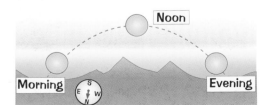

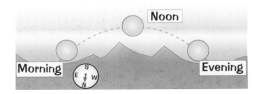

Long shadows in winter — and long faces...

The Earth orbits the Sun in one *year*, — giving us the seasons. Don't get muddled up with the earth spinning to give us night and day. Remember that the sun is *lower* in the sky in *winter* and so the shadows are *longer*. (Look back at P. 88 for the stuff about shadows). Think about the length of the days in winter and summer, too.

Displaying Your Results

Results in Graphs and Charts

Graphs and charts *display* your results like a picture. They have *two axes (we say one axis, two axes)* and it is important to know *what each axis shows* and also the *scale on the axis*.

This graph plots the height of plant in the pots A, B, C and D.

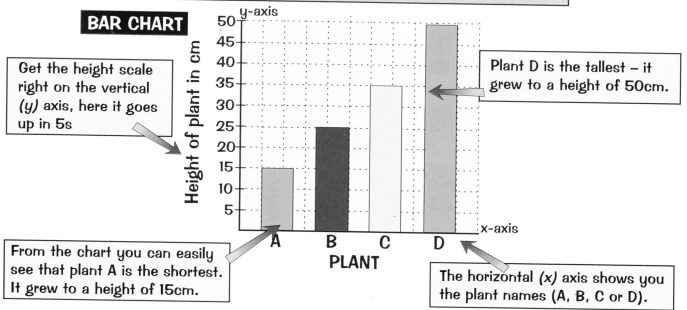

BAR CHART

Get the height scale right on the vertical *(y)* axis, here it goes up in 5s

Plant D is the tallest – it grew to a height of 50cm.

From the chart you can easily see that plant A is the shortest. It grew to a height of 15cm.

The horizontal *(x)* axis shows you the plant names (A, B, C or D).

The graph shows that:

As the pot size increases — the height of the plant also increases.

Graphs can be used to make Predictions

This graph plots the height of plant against the pot size.

Predict how high a plant will grow in an 8cm pot...

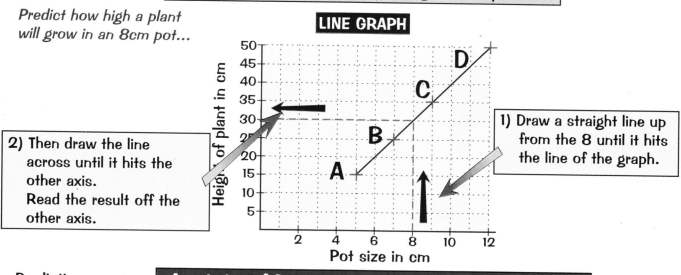

LINE GRAPH

1) Draw a straight line up from the 8 until it hits the line of the graph.

2) Then draw the line across until it hits the other axis. Read the result off the other axis.

Prediction:

A pot size of 8cm — means a plant height of 30cm.

Line graphs — number one in the charts

These are ways of showing your results that show what's been happening even more clearly. It's really important to be able to *read* a graph properly — that means *learning* this stuff...

My Conclusions

An Experiment ends with a Conclusion

1) The *conclusion* is a sentence that *sums up* the *findings* of the *experiment*. It should be related to the aim of the experiment.
2) You can often write your conclusion very simply. You need to explain how *one thing alters* as *another* thing *is changed*.
3) *DO NOT* just describe your results.

In our example experiment —

The larg*er* the pot, the tall*er* the plant   ✓   Good good good

"A big pot produces a big plant"   ✗   Bad bad bad

Use an ....er Word

If you think that saying "......er" in tests is bad news — think again. Examiners are very into "_____er" words.

Just look at these examples of snappy conclusions:

> The tight*er* the string the high*er* the note.
> The quick*er* you stir it, the fast*er* it dissolves.
> The hard*er* you hit the drum, the loud*er* it sounds.
> The hott*er* the temperature, the quick*er* the ice melts.
> The more you wind up the clockwork mouse, the furth*er* it goes.
> The more pocket money you get, the great*er* the amount you spend....

Make your Conclusion Snappy

When you're asked how a thing depends on something else, or how something affects something else, then it's time to produce a snappy conclusion like this one...

Did someone say snappy...

The bett*er* you learn this — the high*er* the number of marks you'll get.

Don't let these conclusions cause you any confusion...

It's really all about spotting a pattern in your results and saying what it is in a way that everyone can understand. Remember it's much *better to write* "The bigger the pot the taller the plant" *than* "A big pot produces a big plant". The first answer covers *all* the possibilities and will get you *more marks* — so use "_____er" words or words like more or less. If you just talk about a *big* pot, I won't know *how* big you mean, you see.

SECTION THIRTEEN — DOING AN EXPERIMENT

Summary Questions For Section Thirteen

This section of the book is a bit different from the others. The first few pages of the section is mainly *facts* — unfortunately, you just have to learn these, but there are some examples for you to chew on. You'll have to be able to apply what you learn here to lots of different things. There are always loads of questions in the tests which involve *filling in tables, reading tables* and *reading graphs and charts*. Practice on the examples in the text and then try the questions. Don't forget *PRACTICE MAKES PERFECT* (he said meaninglessly)

1) What is the *"aim"* of an experiment?

2) How would you make sure an experiment was a *fair test?*

3) If you wanted to find out how long it took salt to dissolve at *different temperatures*, what would you do to make this a *fair test?*

4) What *equipment* would you use to find out how hot a beaker of water is? What *units* would you use for the answer?

5) What *measuring instrument* would you use to find out how long it takes for sugar to dissolve? What *units* would you use for the answer?

6) What are the *units of mass?* What would you use to *measure* mass?

7) Some children did an experiment to find out *how quickly an ice cube melts*. At first it weighed 50g. After 5 minutes it weighed 30g, after 10 minutes 20g, after 15 minutes 10g and after 20 minutes it had completely gone. Put these results into the *table* opposite. Some results are done for you.

		Weight in grammes
		50g
Time in minutes	5	
		20g
	10	10g
	20	

8) Class 5 did an experiment to find which type of battery worked best. They tested 4 different batteries in the same torch to see which lasted longest. They plotted their results on a bar chart.

a) Which battery lasted *longest?*

b) Which battery worked *least well?*

c) How long did the *"Mr. Average"* battery last?

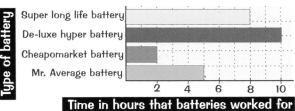

9) An experiment was carried out with a wooden block and several slopes of 1 metre in length, but at different heights. The block was sent down each slope in turn and the distance it travelled beyond the end of the slope was measured. This was done to see if changing the height of the slope altered the distance the block travelled.

a) Can you predict *how far* the block would travel if the starting height of the slope was *10cm?*

b) *How far* does the block travel when the starting height of the slope is *0cm? Why?*

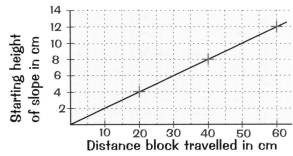

Write simple conclusions for the next 2 questions.

— If you are stuck, turn to the relevant section in this guide.

10) How will the *temperature* in a room affect the rate at which an ice cube melts?

11) How does the *position of the sun* in the sky affect the length of the shadow of a tree?

Answers

Section One

1) Movement, reproduction, sensitivity, nutrition, excretion, respiration and growth.
2) MRS NERG.
3) It is doing all seven life processes.
4) True.
5) Both do the seven life processes.
6) Reproduction.
7) Oxygen.
8) Excretion.
9) They notice changes in their surroundings and react to them. Babies and seedlings get bigger and turn into adults.
10) Cells.
11) Cells.
12) True.
13) a) living b) dead c) never lived d) dead e) dead f) living g) dead h) never lived.

Section Two

1) Leaves, roots, stem, flower.
2) Animals have to eat to get food, plants make their own.
3) Making something out of light. Plants make food by photosynthesis.
4) Carbon dioxide is used up.
5) Oxygen is made.
6) In the leaves.
7) Most happens in the day.
8) Water and minerals.
9) To help them grow well.
10) In the flower.
11) A pollen grain.
12) Pollination.
13) Pollination happens first.
14) Wind blowing pollen onto the stigma, or insects carrying pollen to the stigma.
15) Scent and bright coloured petals.
16) Nectar.
17) They don't need to attract insects.
18) Small, dull, not scented.
19) To help pollen stick to it.
20) Fertilisation.
21) The flower dies and falls off.
22) The ovary becomes a fruit.
23) Dispersal prevents overcrowding.
24) By the wind, by animals or by exploding.
25) It splits open and the seeds shoot out.
26) Seeds are made in the flower.
27) A seed staring to grow.
28) Water, warmth and air.
30) Seeds don't need light to germinate.

Section Three

2) Oxygen and food.
3) Lungs and kidneys.
4) Inside the body.
5) For support, to protect delicate organs, to allow movement.
6) Tendons.
7) Ligaments.
8) It relaxes.
9) Veins, arteries, capillaries.
10) Capillaries.
11) The heart.
12) The blood takes oxygen away and gives carbon dioxide back.
13) Arteries.
14) The windpipe.
15) A heart beat.
16) About 70.
17) Incisors, canines and molars.
18) a) incisors b) molars c) canines.
19) a) eats plants and animals b) eats animals c) eats plants.
20) Milk teeth.
21) Sticky slime on the teeth caused by bacteria eating sugar in the mouth.
22) Enamel.
23) Four from: Brushing teeth twice a day, flossing teeth, drinking water with fluoride, visiting the dentist regularly, eating the right foods.
24) Baby, child, adolescent, adult.
25) Boys: Hair grows on body, hair grows on face, testicles start producing sperm.
    Girls: hair grows on body, breasts develop, hips widen, Ovaries start to release eggs, menstruation (periods) begin.
26) Monthly loss of blood from the uterus.
27) Starches, sugars, proteins, fats, vitamins, fibre and water.
28) Fats and carbohydrates.
29) Exercise strengthens the muscles, develops the lungs, helps body co-ordination, uses up food and can help you sleep.
30) Smoking causes lung cancer, alcohol damages the liver.
31) Germs.
32) Bacteria and viruses.
33) Yeast is used to make bread and beer, some bacteria are used to make vinegar, cheese and yoghurt.
34) Flu, chicken pox, tetanus, polio, AIDS etc.
35) Wash hands before handling food, store raw meat away from cooked meat, store food in a refrigerator, heat food properly when cooking, keep food covered.
36) Wash your hands after you have been to the toilet. Don't cough or sneeze over people.
37) Vaccinations and antibiotics.

Section Four

2) Animals and plants.
3) Vertebrates and invertebrates.
4) With a backbone.
5) Fish, amphibians, reptiles, birds and mammals.
6) Insects, Arachnids and Molluscs.
7) a) fish b) birds c) reptiles d) mammals e) amphibian.
8) Birds and mammals.
9) Reptiles, amphibians and fish.
10) Mammals.
11) Insects.
12) Spider: 8 legs and 2 body sections. Ant: 6 legs and 3 body sections.
13) Flowering and non-flowering.
14) Spores.
15) Evergreen.
16) In cones.
17) They fall off in winter.
18) Ash, Oak, Beech, Birch, Willow etc.

Answers

Section Five

1) Habitat.
2) Food, shelter and somewhere to bring up children.
3) Eyes and nostrils close underwater, webbed feet, long whiskers.
4) A bushy tail helps it balance in the treetops.
5) Long roots, fleshy stems and thin leaves (needles).
6) One from: Streamlined body, small ears, layers of fat, oily fur or webbed feet.
7) One from: Long tail and large toes, large ears, thin fur, active at night.
8) Streamlined body, gills, fins, sensitive areas to detect movement and smell food.
9) Eyes and nostrils above water, webbed feet, powerful back legs, moist skin, wide mouth and sticky tongue.
10) Bristles for grip, moist skin, pointed head.
11) Flat body, protective plates, big antennae.
12) a) leaf b) 3 c) bird, worm, cat d) bird e) worm f) bird g) cat h) cat i) bird, cat.
13) "Is food for."
14) Prey.
15) Predators.
16) A food web.

Section Six

1) Different useful properties.
2) It is strong.
3) It is flexible.
4) Plastic — lightweight, strong, easily shaped, waterproof.
5) Plastic cups, some toys, plastic food containers etc.
6) ...Of materials.
7) Coal, oil, rock, metal.
8) Man made.
9) Crockery, bricks.
10) Glass, recycled paper.
11) b
12) Metals.
13) Something that won't let heat pass through it easily.
14) Metals.
15) b
16) Shaped easily, floats, strong but pliable, electrical insulator, thermal insulator.
17) Light, but difficult to get rid of.
18) Fibres.
19) It is synthetic.
20) Glass.
21) In the ground, mixed in with rocks.
22) Strong and tough, shiny, easily shaped, make a noise when hit, can be recycled, some are magnetic, conductors of heat and electricity.
23) Iron, copper, tin, aluminium, zinc, brass etc.
24) Some are harder, some are permeable.
25) Ground up rock, humus, air and water.
26) Lets water pass through.
27) Solids, liquids, gases.
28) The tiny bits that everything's made of.
29) A gas.
30) I am runny. I take the shape of the container I'm poured into.

Section Seven

1) It dissolves.
2) A mixture of a solid and a liquid, when the solid is dissolved in the liquid to make a new liquid.
3) Add more water.
4) The oil would float on the water. They won't mix.
5) Some of the soil sinks to the bottom and some floats around in the water.
6) Liquid.
7) Baking a cake, burning wood etc.
8) It turns into a solid.
9) Thermometer.
10) Thermometer.
11) a) 100°C b) 0°C.
12) False (it would be frozen solid). Degrees below freezing.
13) Ice, water, steam.
14) Ice takes up more room than water.
15) There is a very thin "skin" on the water surface.
16) Tiny water droplets suspended in the air.
17) Steam is very hot and is invisible.
18) They evaporate as it gets warmer.
19) Leave the solution in a wide dish in a warm place.
20) False. A gas condenses into a liquid when it is cooled.
21) Water evaporates from the sea, condenses and falls as rain over the land and runs back down to the sea.
22) b
23) Water freezing, ice cream melting.
24) They rot.
25) Wood, coal, oil, gas, charcoal, etc...
26) Food.
27) They must burn.

Section Eight

1) a) filter paper b) magnet c) sieve d) spoon (with heat).
2) Decanting.
3) Yes...but not that way round! Magnet attracts nails.
4) On top of the sand.
5) Round.
6) A cone shape.
7) The mud can't get through the tiny gaps in the cloth.
8) Tea leaves stay inside. Tea flavour dissolves in water and comes out.
9) Sugar, salt.
10) Insoluble.
11) The sugar or salt is dissolved in the water.
12) Heat the solution and evaporate the salt. Condense the water if you want.
13) Tea flavour passes through, tea leaves stays behind.
14) Evaporate of the water.
15) Cold surface.
16) a)
17) Chromatography.

Section Nine

1) Light bulbs, television, radios, washing machine, iron etc.
2) It makes them portable – you can carry them around.
3) Safety – you will get an electric shock.
4) The water on your hands conducts electricity very well.
5) So you can't touch the switch with wet hands.
6) To conduct the electricity.

Answers

7) To insulate.

8) So if there is a fault, they'll be insulated.

9) Electricity will not flow.

10) Yes.

11) Bulb, buzzer, motor.

12) Both wires connected to same end of battery. Wire touching glass of bulb, not metal bit. Only one wire to bulb or battery. Bulb is dead, battery is dead.

13) No current.

16) When there's a short-cut for current, so it doesn't flow through the bulb.

17) It makes a gap in the cicuit to switch off and joins up again to switch on.

18) Off.

20) Bulb brighter.

21) Bulb blows.

22) Fewer batteries, more bulbs, longer wire.

Section Ten

1) Push and pull.

2) Change direction, speed up, change shape, slow down.

3) Newtons.

4) Newtonmeter or spring balance.

5) Force between things that are touching.

6) Smooth.

7) Friction.

8) To stop us falling over and to help us start and stop moving.

9) Rough.

10) Heat.

11) Force of the air pushing back as something moves through it.

12) Streamlined.

13) Parachute - it has a large surface area.

14) Gravity. No, it's felt everywhere.

15) Beat their wings.

16) Push back.

17) Gravity and upthrust.

18) Force of air or water or solid object pushing up, depends on how much water has been pushed away by the object.

19) The boat pushes away more water.

20) It displaces more water so the upthrust from the water is enough to balance the force of gravity.

21) Upthrust and gravity.

22) Neither will move.

23) Because the pull of gravity will be greater than the upthrust acting on you, and you will fall!

24) Like poles repel.

25) Opposite poles attract.

Section Eleven

1) Candle, torch, sun.

2) The light reflects off the smooth surface.

3) b

5) Opaque object gets in the way.

6) Place hand close to the light.

7) Smaller.

8) Midday.

9) No light gets through. Wood.

10) Light can pass through, but you can't see through it. Tupperware.

11) You can see through it. Glass.

12) Light bounces off the shiny surface.

13) Smooth and shiny.

14) Dull and dark.

16) Periscope.

17) The same.

18) Something vibrates.

19) Air, water, glass, brick, stone.

20) Vacuum – nothing to vibrate.

21) Something vibrates – air vibrates – ear-drum vibrates.

22) Small.

23) How high or low it is.

24) The thing vibrating – the air in the bottle – is shorter.

25) Twang it hard.

26) Make it tighter.

Section Twelve

1) The sun.

2) Sun's gravity.

3) Spherical.

4) The Sun, 1 year.

5) The Earth, 28 days.

6) Sun, Earth, Moon.

7) Weaker.

8) You can't always see the side that's in the sun.

9) Between Sun and Earth or when it's above the opposite side of the Earth, e.g. Australia.

10) Round on its axis and around the Sun.

11) 1 day.

12) The Sun shines on one part of the Earth.

13) No.

14) It stays at the centre of the solar system.

15) It rises in the east, sets in the west.

16) Midday, Sun high in the sky.

17) We get seasons.

18) Summer.

19) Sun is lower in the sky and days are shorter.

20) Summer.

21) Winter, the Sun is low in the sky.

Section Thirteen

1) Aim – the purpose of an experiment. What you're supposed to find out.

2) You would only change one variable at a time.

3) You would use the same amount of salt and same amount of water each time.

4) Thermometer, °C.

5) Stopwatch, seconds.

6) Grams/kilograms - a balance.

8) a) Deluxe b) cheapo c) five hours.

9) a) 50cm.
   b) It wouldn't slide down because the slope is flat.

10) The warmer it is the faster the ice cube will melt.

11) The higher the sun is in the sky, the shorter the shadow.

Index

Index